Profiling
Violent
Crimes

Ronald M. Holmes · Stephen T. Holmes
Second Edition

Profiling
Violent
Crimes
An Investigative Tool

SAGE Publications
International Educational and Professional Publisher
Thousand Oaks   London   New Delhi

For information address:

 SAGE Publications, Inc.
2455 Teller Road
Thousand Oaks, California 91320
E-mail: order@sagepub.com

SAGE Publications Ltd.
6 Bonhill Street
London EC2A 4PU
United Kingdom

SAGE Publications India Pvt. Ltd.
M-32 Market
Greater Kailash I
New Delhi 110 048 India

Printed in the United States of America

Library of Congress Cataloging-in-Publication Data

Holmes, Ronald M.
    Profiling violent crimes: An investigative tool / authors, Ronald
M. Holmes, Stephen T. Holmes.—2nd ed.
        p.   cm.
    Includes bibliographical references and index.
    ISBN 0-8039-7238-5 (cloth: acid-free).—ISBN 0-8039-7239-3
(pbk.: acid-free)
    1. Criminal investigation—Psychological aspects.   2. Criminal
behavior—Research—Methodology.   3. Criminal methods—Research—
Methodology—Case studies.   I. Holmes, Stephen T.   II. Title.
HV8073.5.H65   1996
363.2′5—dc20   95-32539

This book is printed on acid-free paper.

96 97 98 99   10 9 8 7 6 5 4 3 2 1

Sage Production Editor: Astrid Virding
Sage Typesetter: Andrea D. Swanson

Contents

Preface and Acknowledgments

Within the past 15 years there has been increasing interest in psychological profiling. If profiling had ever been expected to resolve all difficulties in bringing to justice the perpetrators of violent personal crimes, it would have to be classified as an abject failure. In its role as yet another forensic tool to complement thorough investigation by competent and educated law enforcement professionals, however, it can be very useful.

Profiling has been practiced on many levels for years. Hitler was profiled in the latter days of World War II. The Boston Strangler and Mad Bomber were both profiled, with different degrees of accuracy. Fictional murderers have maintained the popularity of profiling for years. Such detectives as Sherlock Holmes, Charlie Chan, and Will Graham, the retired federal agent in Thomas Harris's novel *The Red Dragon* (1981), are as popular today as ever before. Law enforcement agencies are beginning to recognize the possible benefits of profiling. Over the past several years, I have been involved as a profiler in more than 425 homicide and rape cases, almost all of which were submitted by police agencies (a few were referred to me by prosecuting attorneys and even defense attorneys). Although this

may appear to be a sign of the faith and confidence these professionals have in my ability, I must add that the same people have often
sought the advice of astrologers and psychics before they consulted
a sociopsychological profiler. So much for faith in this new "art."

When I profiled my first murder case, I tried to combine my
knowledge of the social and behavioral sciences. I resisted the
temptation to be an academic homicide detective. The first profile
was amazingly accurate, and I caught the bug. The killer was
apprehended, not as a result of my profile but as a result of luck.

As I continued my profiling activities, I realized that there was a
lack of sources available to aid in the training of profilers. What was
available was an atmosphere of mystery and mysticism surrounding
the process of profiling violent criminals. I heard more than a few
police officers voice a desire to "sit at the feet of the masters" to
learn all there is to know about the art of profiling.

I decided to take a different approach. I decided to work back-
ward, so to speak. When you want to know about violent crime, why
not go to the violent offenders? I talked and corresponded with
violent personal offenders, rapists, and murderers. I asked them
questions about their crimes, motivations, and crime scenes. I combined the knowledge I gained from those in prison, often on death
row, with theoretical knowledge and my own practical experience.

This book, which describes the basic elements of profiling, is a
product of that endeavor. It is not a cook book—it will not turn
anyone into a profiler. What it will do is acquaint readers with the
general principles of profiling, as well as what they need to be able
to develop sociopsychological profiles. I believe that experience, a
thorough knowledge of the social and behavioral sciences (including
criminology), and a knowledge of police investigative techniques
serve as a firm base for learning about profiling.

Note that I use the term *sociopsychological profiling* rather than
psychological profiling. I attach the prefix *socio* because what a
thorough profile offers is more than a personality sketch. A thorough
profile includes social demographic data, which are not usually part
of the classic definition of psychological profiling. Age, race, sex,
occupation, education, and other factors make up the *social core*

variables addressed in the profiling process. Because *sociopsy-chological* is a rather large and unwieldy word, in this volume we refer often simply to psychological profiling. The reader should keep in mind that, as we use the term, *psychological profiling* includes social demographic elements.

Since the first edition of this book was published, much has changed. For one thing, in this edition we have made the conscious decision not to include a chapter on Satanic murders, as was offered in the first edition, for several reasons. First of all, even though we believe that the profiling information offered in that chapter was accurate, we have become dismayed by the number of persons who have made careers out of advancing false accusations of a Satanic underground that is supposedly responsible for thousands of murders yearly. We have found no evidence that this is true. There are a few murders committed each year that have overtones of Satanism, mostly by individuals who are not members of any organized Satanic church. Rather, these persons may be better understood as dabblers who do not understand the dogmas of real Satanists. In addition, the information in the first edition's chapter on Satanism was geared toward identifying suspects' involvement in Satanism and its influence on the commission of crimes, and we believe there has been a general decline in the commission of crimes linked with Satanism.

Further changes in this edition include chapters on geoforensic analysis and the use of computers for psychological profiling. Kim Rossmo, coauthor of Chapter 10, has conducted research that has produced exciting information on geography as it applies to offenders' nodes of behavior, activity space, distance decay function, predator comfort zones, and more. In Chapter 11, we discuss database applications for tracking violent offenders.

This edition also includes two new chapters on arson and pedophilia. These are important if for no other reason than the sheer number of cases of these crimes reported to the criminal justice system. The chapter on arson is bound to stimulate the criticism that we have misplaced a chapter on property crime in a book on violent personal crimes. However, we will take the heat for this inclusion. First, we believe it belongs here because of the danger to which arsonists expose vulnerable victims. Second, it is our position that not all arsonists are alike, and that for some there is a sexual component to fire setting. I used a similar argument when I decided to include a chapter on rape in the first edition. It is widely accepted, although some may disagree, that rape is a crime of violence, with sex the weapon. With the pyromaniac, an eroticized motive accompanies the criminal act. We believe that arson in general, and pyromania in particular, is a property crime that may include violent personal crime, and that arsonists are suitable subjects for profiling. This is also the position of the profilers who work in the Behavioral Science Unit of the Federal Bureau of Investigation.

Aside from adding four new chapters to this edition, we have revised and updated the chapters that appeared in the first edition. For example, we have included new information in the chapters on rape and serial murder, as well as the theoretical chapters. New information arrives daily, not only about the psychological aspects of crime and criminals, but also concerning the scientific aspects of crime scene analysis.

Since the publication of the first edition, I have heard some criticism from criminologists and sociologists about the treatment of theory in this book. However, I have also heard positive remarks from my students, students from other universities, and police officers who use my book about the simple and straightforward manner in which theories are presented. As we point out in the text, the serious student of criminal personality development should of course refer to the works of the originators of these theories (e.g., Merton, 1968; Sutherland, 1937) for fuller understanding. Also, as I say to the people who take my classes and seminars, it is not my mission to explain criminal behavior. It is my mission to look at a crime scenario and offer an educated guess about the offender(s). It is my purpose in this book to share my knowledge about how to do that.

No work of this nature takes place in a vacuum. Special people deserve special thanks: Dr. Al Carlisle, Utah State Prison; Jerry Thompson, Salt Lake County (Utah) Sheriff's Department; Norman Pomrenke, former director of the Southern Police Institute; Bob Crouse, Southern Police Institute; Jim Massie, Kentucky Parole

Office; Don Patchen, Tallahassee Police Department; Sergeant David Rivers, Metro-Dade (Florida) Police Department; Corporal Jay F. Whitt, Greensboro (North Carolina) Police Department; Lieutenant George Barret, Louisville (Kentucky) Police Department; Sheriff Charles Cox, Miami (Ohio) Sheriff's Office; Eric Hickey, California State University at Fresno; Steve Egger, Sangamon State University; and Jack Levin, Northeastern University. If there are others whom I have neglected to list, I hope they understand.

In addition, I have also gained a great deal of insight into crimes of a violent nature from offenders themselves. Ted Bundy, Doug Clark, and others have given me tremendous insight into the minds of the very violent. Other incarcerated offenders to whom I have written, and who have corresponded with me across prison walls, have given me more insight into the criminal mind than can be gleaned from any academic textbook. There is one particular offender who is in a maximum security institution; this admitted rapist and murderer has helped me gain insight that has been invaluable in my analysis of violent crimes. I sincerely believe that without the help of this one special person, who has been willing to open his soul despite the pain it has caused him, this work would have been greatly limited. But I also believe he has shared his thoughts because this is the only way he could help those he has raped and injured, and the families of those he has killed. In letters to me, he has detailed his thoughts about victimization; these have proven to be valuable for my own understanding of the mind of the predator, and, more important, have alerted law enforcement personnel to crime scene elements that may offer details about certain social core variables of unknown offenders.

It is my sincere hope that the information in this book will aid those who must investigate various types of predatory crimes. If it helps in just one case, then it was indeed worth the effort.

                                                                    Ronald M. Holmes

1. Psychological Profiling

An Introduction

Historically, crime and criminals have galvanized the attention of law-abiding citizens. Whatever the reason, be it the "romance" of a Capone or a Dillinger or the utter lack of understanding of how or why criminals can do what they do, books, television, and movies flood the market with police and crime. Unlike in a vintage *Dragnet* episode, however, Joe Friday does not always bring the criminal to justice. Every killer is not peacefully arrested based on nothing more than his or her MO (*modus operandi,* or method of operation)—the "signature" of the perpetrator. The basic principle behind the identification of an MO is that each perpetrator supposedly commits crimes in a certain manner. Therefore, each time a person commits a crime, he or she will do so in the same—or at least similar—fashion. This is a prodigious step in logic, but one that has been "validated" by tradition and common sense, both less-than-reliable sources of knowledge.

For homicide investigators who must deal with cases where the motives of "normal" killings are absent, psychological profiling may be an essential investigative tool (Douglas & Burgess, 1986; Douglas, Burgess, Burgess, & Ressler, 1992; Palmiotto, 1994; Sears, 1991). A psychological profile represents "an educated attempt to provide investigative agencies with specific information as to the type of individual who committed a certain crime" (Geberth, 1981, p. 46).

Of course, profiling is not a suitable tool for all cases, even in some murder cases (Holmes & Holmes, 1992). Profiles are usually most efficacious in cases where an unknown perpetrator has displayed indications of psychopathology (Holmes & Holmes, 1994). According to our own research and that of others (e.g., Geberth, 1993), the types of crimes most appropriate for psychological profiling are as follows:

- Sadistic torture in sexual assaults
- Evisceration
- Postmortem slashing and cutting
- Motiveless fire setting
- Lust and mutilation murder
- Rape
- Satanic and ritualistic crime
- Pedophilia

It is important to come to a general understanding of the types of persons who would commit such crimes. Inherent within the premise of the validity and reliability of a profile is that the person who, for example, commits a lust murder has a personality that reflects pathology. Chaos, lack of planning, mutilation, and so on all reflect the killer's personality. Therefore, the crime scene itself reflects pathology. It is the responsibility of the profiler to offer insights from the physical evidence of the pathology exhibited in the crime scene (Michaud, 1986).

GOALS IN PROFILING

In the following, we delineate the goals of profiling; we consider these to be broad statements of what profiling is intended to accomplish. Our description of goals is intended to be general; we do not offer here the specific objectives of profiling, or "measurable statements of what we want to accomplish by a given point of time" (Craig, 1980, p. 24).

The three major goals of profiling are to provide the criminal justice system with the following:

1. Social and psychological assessments of offenders
2. Psychological evaluations of belongings found in the possession of suspected offenders
3. Suggestions and strategies for interviewing suspected offenders when they are apprehended

GOAL 1: SOCIAL AND PSYCHOLOGICAL ASSESSMENTS

A profile should contain basic and sound information concerning the social and psychological core variables of the offender's personality, including the offender's race, age, employment status and type, religion, marital status, and level of education. This psychosocial information will help to focus the investigation by allowing police to narrow its range, which in turn will have a direct effect upon the number of days and weeks police must spend on the case.

The social and psychological assessment within a profile should contain information that can alert law enforcement professionals to the possible psychological traits of a perpetrator revealed in a crime scene. A carefully prepared profile may predict future possible attacks as well as the probable sites of those attacks.

Case study: A profile was completed for a police department in a southern city, where, in the course of 4 months, four young women had been murdered, their throats cut. None of the women had been sexually molested, and there were several other commonalities among the crimes. The profile offered information as to the probable age, level of education, and residence of the perpetrator, and a predicted period of time within which he would likely strike again. The profile was accurate, even to the day the next attack would occur. The police department, with confidence in the profiling packet, redoubled their efforts, with the positive benefit that the attacker was apprehended on the night his next attack was predicted.

GOAL 2: PSYCHOLOGICAL EVALUATION OF BELONGINGS

When investigators have a prime suspect, they can gain a great deal from a profile that provides them with a psychological evaluation of the suspect's belongings. It may be that all of the physical evidence, witness reports, and other pertinent information point toward one suspect, but the police may need help in understanding how certain possessions may tie the suspect to the crime. The psychological profile should suggest any particular items an offender may have in his or her possession, such as crime scene souvenirs, photos, pornography, or other items that serve as reminders of the violent episode.

Case study: Jerry Brudos is a serial killer currently in Oregon State Penitentiary for the brutal and sadistic killing of young women in the late 1960s. Brudos has a shoe fetish. He had stolen a pair of high-heeled black shoes during the course of a robbery and rape, and often wore the shoes around his home and demanded his wife do the same. Brudos forced one victim, a young National Merit scholar, to wear the shoes even as he hung her from the rafters in his garage. In addition, Brudos was involved in triolism, a sexual behavior in which sexual gratification is gained by seeing oneself and/or others in sexual scenes. Combining his transvestism with triolism, Brudos took pictures of himself wearing the high-heeled shoes, panties, bra, and stockings. He also took pictures of his wife nude, and photographed three of his four victims. One victim was already dead when he photographed her. (Stack, 1983)

If profiling had been used by the police department that investigated Brudos's crimes, such a profile might have alerted the police to the possibility that they might find "souvenirs" or "trophies" (such as the shoes and photographs) in the perpetrator's possession. Such physical evidence, if listed on a search warrant, could have been invaluable material to be used in his trial. Also, with such a profile, police may have been alerted to the possibility that the perpetrator would photograph his victims, and so could have investigated whether any suspicious photos had been developed recently through local businesses. As it happened, Brudos had convinced his wife that she could pose for him in the nude and he could safely get the pictures developed because "big labs process too much film to look at every picture. . . . They look at the first or the last—and that's all" (Stack, 1983, p. 33). He apparently used this same subjective rationale when he photographed his victims.

GOAL 3: INTERVIEWING SUGGESTIONS AND STRATEGIES

The third goal of profiling is to offer the police information regarding the proper and effective methods for interviewing or interrogating a particular offender once he or she has been apprehended. This can be crucial. The profile packet should include suggestions for the most effective strategies for eliciting information from this particular offender, based on the information in the rest of the profile. Not all people react to questioning in the same fashion. For one type of offender, one strategy may be effective, but it is a mistake to assume that all those who commit similar crimes will respond to the same interviewing strategy. For example, not all serial murderers kill for the same reasons, and not all respond to the same type of interviewing strategy. Violent personal offenders also vary in their motives as well as their responses to interrogation.

Case study: In a small midwestern town, 15-year-old Diana Harris and her boyfriend were shot. Their bodies were found in the boyfriend's car, parked in a lonely "lover's lane" area. Diana died of one shot to the left temple; her male companion was also shot once, the bullet entering under his left armpit. One additional bullet was fired through the car's passenger-side window. No physical evidence other than the bullets was obtained at the crime scene.

The police department investigated the case thoroughly but unsuccessfully. After talking with Diana's mother and stepfather, one detective believed that the stepfather was not telling all that he knew. Most people feared Mr. Harris, who was a football coach. He carried himself in a way that defied anyone to doubt his virility, masculinity, or intelligence.

The detective decided to reinterview the stepfather about the case. After questioning Harris for several hours, the detective asked him pointedly if he had killed his stepdaughter and her boyfriend. Breaking into profuse perspiration, Harris replied, "Not in my right mind did I kill them. You'll have to prove that I did." At that point, instead of keeping up the pressure, the detective took a break from the questioning. After the break, and a chance to regroup psychologically, Harris denied any knowledge or responsibility in the case. All progress stopped, and the investigation came to a halt. No matter what strategy they used, the police were unable to get any more information from Harris.

Finally, the police department requested outside help concerning the direction of Harris's interrogation. The consultant, who suspected that Harris had a strong need to be in control, suggested a new strategy. The suspect was taken into an interrogation room in which pictures of the crime scene lined the four walls, serving as constant reminders of what had occurred. There he was told that the police really wanted to solve the crime of the murder of his stepdaughter, but, despite all their work, they were getting nowhere. They asked for his help. Harris, believing he was now in control of the investigation and in a position to offer some helpful suggestions to the police, became fully engrossed in talking about the case. The more he talked, the more he revealed his familiarity with the details of the crime. After more than 8 hours, he broke down and cried. When the detective then resumed his questioning, Harris confessed to the double homicide.

PROFILING: AN ART, NOT A SCIENCE

Not everyone agrees that psychological profiling is of benefit to law enforcement (Jenkins, 1994). Campbell (1976), a psychologist, has argued that professionals in criminal justice must realize that profiling is at best an art, not a science. He maintains that (a) the profiles submitted to police departments as gospel concerning the types of offenders who commit violent acts are probably little better than the information one could obtain from the neighborhood bartender, (b) profiles are either too vague and ambiguous or no more than simple common sense, and (c) as long as police officers are impressed with the credentials, status, and education of academicians, many academicians will continue to play their educational guessing games. Vernon Geberth, a retired homicide commander with the New York Police Department, recently told us that he was misquoted in a 1994 *Miami Herald* article as saying that he was not aware of one serial murder case where a profile led to an arrest. Geberth told us that the actual quote should have been as follows: "Criminal profiling is an excellent law enforcement tool. However, it is just one of many tools and does not replace good investigative techniques. In fact, I don't know of any profile in and by itself that has resulted in an actual arrest" (personal communication, February 6, 1995). Although there may be some truth to the criticisms cited above, it is reasonable to expect that a profiler's years of education and training will be of value to law enforcement officials in their attempts to solve difficult crimes.

There are a few rules that all profilers should obey in creating profiles related to difficult criminal cases. Of course, profilers make educated guesses—such guesses are, however, aided by the knowledge profilers have gained from experience in the criminal justice system and from familiarity with relevant concepts in criminology, sociology, psychology, and psychiatry. In addition, the profiler is aided by an intuitive sense; that is, a good profiler develops a "feel" for certain kinds of crime. This is the art dimension of profiling. Nonprofessional sources of information seldom have the mixture of competencies essential for efficient profiling.

CONCLUSION

The tool of psychological profiling is clearly more suitable for use in certain kinds of cases than in others. The role of the profiler, then, is to assist the police in their investigations of those kinds of cases when the police seek additional aid. Successful profilers have a blend of educational and training backgrounds that allow them to offer insights into the types of persons who commit certain kinds of crimes. The profile itself, however, is more than a simple list of suspected characteristics. The goals of the profiler are threefold: A complete profile provides the criminal justice system with (a) a social and psychological assessment of the offender, (b) a psychological evaluation of the suspected offender's belongings, and (c) suggestions for the most efficient and effective way for police to go about interviewing the suspect once he or she is apprehended. A profiler's ability to attain these goals may be described as both art and science.

2. Profiling in Fantasy and Fact

Crime has long been an interest of popular readers. Since the mid-1800s, Sir Arthur Conan Doyle, G. K. Chesterton, Agatha Christie, Earl Biggers, Lawrence Sanders, Thomas Harris, and others have written novels that have influenced readers' impressions of the exploration of criminals and their crimes.

SHERLOCK HOLMES: THE MASTER DETECTIVE

In the late 1800s, a fictional master detective contributed his delving mind to police departments and citizens alike in the solving of particularly puzzling crimes. Accompanied by his good friend and associate Dr. Watson, Sherlock Holmes solved case after case, rarely failing. This point is illustrated in Holmes's dialogue with a young wife who, in one story, asks his help:

Wife: He [Major Prendergast] said that you could solve anything.
Holmes: He said too much.
Wife: That you are never beaten.

9

> *Holmes:* I have been beaten four times—three times by men, and once by a woman.
>
> *Wife:* But what is that compared with the number of your successes?
>
> *Holmes:* It is true that I have been generally successful. (Doyle, 1891c, p. 70)

Holmes solved his cases by deduction, and by seeing things others failed to notice. Watson was constantly amazed by what Holmes was able to observe:

> But I was always oppressed with a sense of my own stupidity in my dealings with Sherlock Holmes. Here I had heard what he had heard, I had seen what he had seen, and yet from his words it was evident that he saw clearly not only what had happened, but what was about to happen. (Doyle, 1891d, p. 35)

The consummate detective, Holmes took note of evidence that others neglected. On many occasions, he remarked, "Perhaps I have trained myself to see what others overlook" (Doyle, 1891b, p. 42).

Sherlock Holmes maintained that the educated and trained mind of the detective is the most important forensic tool in the resolution of a crime. The master detective investigated his cases with great care, examining each minute detail. In *The Bascombe Valley Mystery,* for example, Holmes deduces from the manner in which a man has been struck over his left shoulder that the perpetrator is left-handed and walks with a limp. When Holmes explains to Watson how he reached this conclusion, the good doctor is once again astounded by what Holmes has seen and he has not (Doyle, 1891a).

In *The Man With the Twisted Lip,* Holmes investigates the case of a missing husband. One clue centers on the manner in which a letter has been addressed:

> *Holmes:* I perceive also that whoever addressed the envelope had to go and inquire as to the address.
>
> *Mrs. St. Claire:* How can you tell?
>
> *Holmes:* The name, you see, is in perfectly black ink, which has dried itself. The rest is of the grayish color which shows that blotting paper has been used. If it had been written straight off, and then

blotted, none would be of a deep black shade. This man has written the name, and there has then been a pause before he wrote the address, which can only mean that he was not familiar with it. (Doyle, 1892, p. 89)

Holmes amazes not only Watson but also the missing man's wife with this observation. He notes confidently, perhaps arrogantly, that the letter is only a trifle, "but there is nothing so important as trifles" (Doyle, 1892, p. 89).

The gift of Sherlock Holmes is his attention to detail. The physical scene, or the crime scene, is more than simply the site of an accumulation of evidence; there is a synergism that arises from the interaction of offender and scene. A forensic anthropologist may be able to tell the height, weight, and even the race of an offender from a footprint, but a footprint tells nothing of the offender's personality. It is imperative for investigators to examine nonphysical evidence, because it adds to the quality of the scene. From a profiling point of view, both physical and nonphysical evidence can provide clues to an offender's personality.

Holmes never reached the point where he could be described as a psychological profiler. This is due in no small part to the influence of the school of criminology that was in vogue at the time. The *classical school* of criminology, which was quickly followed by the *positive school,* laid the theoretical groundwork for the assumption that humans are in complete control of their actions. Under positive school thinking, people were thought to become criminals because of "savage genes" from their "savage ancestors" or other constitutional factors (Ferrero-Lombroso, 1911). If the psychodynamic model had been better known and accepted at the time, Sherlock Holmes no doubt would have been more heavily involved in the psychological analysis of the criminals he investigated.

WILL GRAHAM AND *THE RED DRAGON*

Thomas Harris has written a terrifying novel about a serial murderer that is more than an exploration of the mind of the killer.

Terrifying and strange, bizarre and compelling, *The Red Dragon*
examines the psychological and mystical relationship between the
killer, Francis Dolarhyde, and his profiler, Will Graham.

As the novel opens, Graham is a retired FBI agent, living in Florida
with his wife and son. Before his retirement, he was involved in a
murder investigation so intense that it resulted in his leaving the
Bureau. However, a friend and former coworker prevails upon him to
come out of retirement to undertake one last case, the case of the Red
Dragon, a serial killer. Harris takes the reader inside the mind of the
profiler as Graham goes to the crime scenes and observes elements
others have missed. Two families have been systematically executed.
In Atlanta, the Leeds family has been killed, both parents and three
children. The children were placed by the killer facing the bed, with
their backs to the wall. The parents were found in their own bed. Mr.
Leeds was bound, tied to the headboard, and his throat slashed.

After examining the Leeds home crime scene, Graham returns to
his motel room, where he mentally reconstructs the crime. Again
and again, he goes over each detail of the scene. The eyes of the
victims were open; Graham thinks, "Were they 'witnesses' to the
killings? Were they an audience?" Recalling a lit candle in the
bedroom, Graham thinks about how its glimmering light may have
served as a visual facilitator of horror. "The flickering light would
simulate expression on their faces" (Harris, 1981, p. 29). Carrying
on a mental conversation with the unknown killer, Graham asks:

> Why did you move them [the children] again? Why didn't you leave
> them that way? There's something you don't want me to know about
> you. Why, there's something you're ashamed of. Or is it something
> you can't afford for me to know?
>   Did you open their eyes?
>   Mrs. Leeds was lovely, wasn't she? You turned on the light after
> you cut his throat so Mrs. Leeds could watch him flop, didn't you?
> It was maddening to have to wear gloves when you touched her,
> wasn't it? (Harris, 1981, p. 29)

Totally immersed in the multiple killings of the two families,
Graham creates a profile of the killer that helps to narrow the scope

of the investigation and provides a structure on which to base an understanding of the killer's personality. With sophisticated police technology, including some techniques that are not currently in the repertoire of real-world forensics, the Red Dragon is eventually brought to justice in a rather unusual way.

No other novel that we know of gives the reader such vivid and realistic insight into the mind of a profiler. Although it is fiction, it illustrates well the introspective nature of profiling—the art as well as the science that profiling requires.

Will Graham becomes personally involved in the Red Dragon case and loses his objectivity. He becomes so intimately involved that he carries on conversations with the perpetrator as well as with the victims. He believes in the need to go to the crime scene because there still lingers a "shadow" of the crime. Photographs, written reports, witness statements, and so on become secondary. This total involvement almost leads to fatal consequences, not only for Graham, but for his wife and son as well.

The Red Dragon provides a fictional introduction to the real world of profiling and to the art involved in the profiler's immersion in a case. In this novel, there is little hard science to the profiling process; Graham proceeds for the most part based on his feelings.

ZOE KOEHLER: A FEMALE SERIAL MURDERER

Lawrence Sanders's (1981) novel *The Third Deadly Sin* is the story of a woman, Zoe Koehler, who has a deep fantasy life that involves the killing of male strangers. Zoe has never really come to terms with her female identity, and there is a hidden part of her personality that no one but her victims has seen. She works as a secretary in a downtown New York hotel, arrives at work each day on time, eats her lunch at her desk, and goes home to an empty apartment. She has felt rejection from all the men in her life: Her father psychologically isolated himself from her in her childhood, and her husband deserted her after only a few years of marriage. The millions of men in New York barely acknowledge her existence.

Zoe's painful menstrual periods announce a metamorphosis in which she changes from a nondescript entity to a killer. She changes from her drab work clothes to seductive clothing, transforming her appearance further with a wig, and travels across town to cocktail lounges at convention sites. (Through her work at the hotel, she is aware of the various conventions in town at any given time.) She allows herself to be picked up and accompanies the man to his room, where he anticipates a sexual encounter. In one such incident, after Zoe and her victim get to his room, she says, "Why don't you take off all those clothes. . . . I have to make wee-wee and then I'll come back to you. I'll do anything you want. And I mean anything" (Sanders, 1981, p. 34). When she returns to the room, after having removed her clothes, she comes to the bed where the man waits, a Swiss Army knife beneath the towel she is carrying. She plunges the knife into the man's neck.

> [The victim] made a sound, a gargle, and his heavy body leaped convulsively from the bed. Blood spouted in streams, gobbets, a flood that sprayed the air with a crimson fog. It soaked the bed, dripped onto the floor.
>
> With bloodied, slippery hand, she drove the knife blade again and again into his genitals. No triumph or exultation in her face. Not grinning or yowling, but intent and businesslike. Saying aloud with each stab, "There. There. There." (p. 34)

Edward X. Delaney, a central figure in several of Sanders's novels, is a retired detective from New York's finest who serves as a special consultant to the police department. Delaney, an amateur profiler, assumes an unofficial posture in investigating the "Hotel Ripper Case." He tells his wife that he suspects the killer is a woman. He says:

> All I'm trying to do is put together a profile. Not a psychological profile—those things are usually pure bullshit. I'm trying to give the killer certain personal and emotional characteristics that give us a more accurate picture of the kind of woman she is. (Sanders, 1981, p. 200)

Despite his protests concerning the nature of profiling, Delaney paints an accurate picture of the Ripper. He pictures her as being from 5 feet, 5 inches to 5 feet, 7 inches tall, "probably a young woman, say in the area of eighteen to forty" (Sanders, 1981, p. 200). How does he come up with this age range? "She's strong enough to rip a man's throat and she's young enough to have menstrual periods" (p. 200). Because the killings occur monthly, 26 days apart, Delaney connects the murders with a woman's menstrual cycle. Using practical reasoning, Delaney continues. He decides she must be intelligent: She carefully plans each act, washes the evidence away, leaves no fingerprints. In addition, he believes the killer dresses conservatively, acts in a conservative fashion, and is probably "mousy. Until she breaks out and kills" (p. 328).

Seeking help from behavioral experts, Delaney constructs a psychological profile that includes many items he had already suspected. There are two additions. First, blood samples show that the killer has Addison's disease. Unless carefully and quickly treated, it will be fatal. Second, the profile suggests the killer is a psychopath, "killing for crazy reasons that maybe don't even make sense to her. But she's forced to kill" (p. 192).

Zoe finally falls in love with a man who accepts her with her faults and her imagined illnesses. However, she still has many self-doubts and continues to kill. Aware that the investigation has identified her as a suspect, Zoe knows time is short and realizes that it will be only a matter of hours before she is caught. Deciding to end her own life, she plans the murder of her lover. Following her same MO, she enters the bedroom as he lies in bed waiting for her and plunges her knife into his throat. Because of her love, however, she does not mutilate his genitals. She then cleans up the bed and herself, puts on her wedding dress, and climbs back into the bed, where she takes an overdose of pills with vodka. The mental pain is stopped, "and for that she was thankful" (Sanders, 1981, p. 407).

Delaney's profile has been accurate. It has led the police to narrow the investigation and finally to obtain an arrest warrant for the murderer. They are too late, however; they find her dead alongside her lover.

Some current novels are also concerned with profiling. In a recent best-seller, *The Alienist* (Carr, 1994), a profile is developed of an unknown child killer. The characters are trying to get inside the mind of the serial killer:

> "I don't understand," I said. "Why would the murderer cut their throats if he'd already strangled them?"
>
> "Blood lust," Marcus answered, very matter-of-factly, as he ate his soup.
>
> "Yes, blood lust," Lucius agreed. "He was probably concerned with keeping his clothes clean so that he wouldn't attract any attention during the escape. He needed to see the blood—or maybe smell it. Some murderers have said it's the smell rather than the sight that satisfies them." (p. 100)

The profile continues: The profilers believe that the killer's mother was unloving, rejecting, and uncaring, and that the killer has some kind of deformity having to do with his eyes. The profile proves accurate, and the killer is eventually brought to justice.

PROFILING IN FACT

The successful resolution of a murder is usually neatly reached by the end of a novel. Sherlock Holmes, Will Graham, and Edward X. Delaney all solved their cases. Unfortunately, profiling in fact does not always yield the same result.

PROFILE OF ADOLPH HITLER

In 1943, the Office of Strategic Services (OSS) sought the help of Dr. Walter C. Langer, a psychiatrist. Dr. Langer, commissioned by Colonel William "Wild Bill" Donovan, was given the task of providing the OSS with

> a realistic appraisal of the German situation. If Hitler is running the show, what kind of person is he? What are his ambitions? . . . We

want to know about his psychological make-up—the things that make him tick. In addition, we ought to know what he might do if things begin to go against him. (Langer, 1972, p. 19)

Langer hired three research assistants who were all familiar with the psychodynamic model. The researchers scoured the New York City Library and their own reading lists, and solicited personal interviews with people who had intimate knowledge of Hitler. Langer's goal was to provide the OSS and Donovan with an objective psychological profile of Adolph Hitler that "might serve as a common basis for decisions in the future" (p. 31).

Aspects of Hitler's profile. From the information available, Langer developed a psychodynamic personality profile of Hitler. According to that profile, Hitler's parents' influence weighed strongly on his future activities. Hitler viewed his father as a distant figure. He was cold, cruel, and brutal in his relationships with his wife and the children. Langer believed that Hitler's mother, on the other hand, was considerate, long-suffering, and overly affectionate, especially to Adolph, who developed a strong libidinal attachment to his mother. He suffered rejection from her, however, because she stayed with her husband instead of leaving him for Adolph. This was to have important implications for the future. In his adult life, Hitler was unable to develop or sustain long-term intimate relationships with males or females because he judged them to be untrustworthy. After all, his father, a male, was cold, sadistic, and inconsiderate. His mother chose not to love him in the same manner in which she loved his father, so she and women in general were not worthy of his trust or love.

Further, according to Langer's profile, Hitler saw himself as an outstanding legal scholar. In addition, despite his failure to gain admission to art school, he considered himself an authority on German architecture.

Like many rulers before him, Hitler believed he was infallible and omnipotent. He believed he had divine protection. A vision empowered him to liberate Germany and make it a world superpower. The war was an answer to his prayers. Psychodynamically speaking, through his leadership he could prove his manhood to his mother by leading Germany once again to victory. When the war started to go badly for Germany, he had to find a scapegoat; the Jews served that purpose well.

Hitler saw himself as a savior. Years before the war, he had envisioned himself as a messiah. When he was in his 20s, he grew a Christlike beard and wanted to be a Catholic priest. During World War II, he likened himself to Christ for the German people.

Benefits of the profile. Langer's profile was intended to offer insights into the personality of Adolph Hitler so that if he was captured at the end of the war, an interrogation strategy would be in place that would help authorities to elicit information from him.

To help the OSS plan for several eventualities, the profile offered several possible scenarios regarding what might become of Hitler at war's end. First, the possibility that Hitler might die of natural causes was quickly dismissed, because he was thought to be in good health. A second possibility was that he could seek refuge in another country, but this was not considered to be likely because he believed that he was indeed the savior of his country. Yet another possibility was that he would be killed in battle. Langer (1972, p. 213) believed that this was a realistic possibility; Hitler might decide to lead his troops into a hopeless battle to glorify his image as a fearless leader.

Another scenario considered the possibility that Hitler might be assassinated. An assassination had been attempted before, so this was not outside the realm of possibility. However, Hitler was very well protected, so this was not considered to be a strong prospect. It was also speculated that Hitler could go insane; Langer believed that Hitler possessed many of the characteristics of a schizophrenic. If the collapse of the Third Reich was indeed at hand, he might deteriorate psychologically. Another possible scenario was that Hitler might be overthrown by German military leaders, such as Rommel, some of whom were not fully committed to Hitler's philosophy. Langer, however, believed that the likelihood of this was remote.

Langer also speculated about the possibility that Hitler could fall into the Allies' hands, but this was considered to be very unlikely. Because of Hitler's personal responsibility for the fate of Germany, it was believed that he would go to extreme lengths to prevent being captured. The most plausible possibility was that if defeat was imminent, Hitler would commit suicide. He had threatened to take his own life on several previous occasions, and had said to Rauschning, "Yes, in the hour of supreme peril I must sacrifice myself for the people" (Langer, 1972, p. 216). Regardless of how the war ended, Langer believed, Hitler's mental condition would worsen. Hitler would fight until he truly believed that the situation was hopeless.

Despite its strong Freudian psychoanalytic orientation, Langer's profile proved to be amazingly accurate as far as the scenarios for the war's end were concerned. Hitler did commit suicide in a bunker with Eva Braun. He never married, perhaps because he never found anyone he felt was enough like his mother. Hitler's writings from the time near the end of the war indicate that he appeared to be on the fringe of mental illness. He also left many documents that pointed toward some unusual sexual leanings: coprolagnia and urolagnia (sexual excitement gained from eating feces and drinking urine) and others. Langer's work was not in vain. It proved to be a worthy attempt at the use of profiling as a tool to understand an aberrant personality.

PROFILE OF A RAPE CASE

Police departments often seek the help of profilers, usually when they have exhausted all of their leads. Recently, a serial rapist terrorized women in a southern city. When the investigators became convinced that they were dealing with a serial rapist, they sought the aid of an outside agency, which studied the crimes and produced "a criminal personality profile." These profilers believed that there were actually two rapists involved in the total of 34 rapes that had been under investigation: One was responsible for 29 rapes and the other for the remaining 5. The main subject of their profile was the

Psychological Profile of the Case of
Ms. Charlene L. Miller by Ronald M. Holmes

Dear Detective Rivers:

Thank you for the opportunity to review the case of Charlene L. Miller. I have reviewed the two-page fact sheet, the pathologic diagnoses of the body document, the forensic anthropologist report, the map of the county and surrounding area, the photos, and the video. I have not talked with you or anyone else about a potential suspect and am offering the following as my general impressions of the type of person you may be looking for as a viable suspect in this case.

Age: The age of this suspect would be in the cohort of 32-36. Perhaps the age could be a couple of years older. There are several reasons for this belief. First of all, I don't see this as the first time this person has done this type of murder. What I am saying is that he has fantasized about killing a woman in this manner for several years. His fantasies have to become real, and for him to do the extent of the acts that he did to this victim takes a long time to finally act out as well as perhaps a murder or two before this particular murder. There are other items which would indicate that he would be about this age: the age of those who would "hang out" in the bars in this community as well as the energy taken in the commission of this crime.

Sex: The sex of the offender is male.

Race: I would believe that this suspect is white. There are several reasons for this. First of all, most murders are committed by persons who are of the same race of the victim. There was not reported any evidence which would indicate that the race of the offender is of any other race than white.

Intelligence: I would think that this person is of average to less-than-average mental ability. I would not believe that this person is a "rocket scientist," but one who would blend in well with the other people he associates with, and probably has the ability to work in jobs with little supervision. I would also think that he is not viewed as mentally retarded but as one who is a loner and one who is viewed by others who know him as being of average ability but a little strange or weird.

Education: This suspect has a high school education or less. Also, while in school he adjusted well and presented no behavioral problems of any significance. He attended a local school in the area of your part of the state. He did not attend college for any significant part of time, and if indeed he did attend college, he stayed less than a semester. His mental ability would not stop him from enrolling into college, but his mental status and personal disorganization would prohibit him from staying in college. In the school situation, he would have been an average student, probably not a behavioral problem.

Family: This person is either an only child or one from a small family with one other sibling. His father was a passive person while the suspect was growing up and may have been deceased or absent from the family. The mother was a domineering person, aggressive, and was the center of power within the family. She was the chief judge, jury, and executioner. Whatever she said was law for the family. I would also believe that she has only recently died, perhaps within the last 6 months. In the family, the child lived under her control, and the mother was constantly verbally abusing the offender.

Residence: At the time of the present murder, the suspect lived in this local area and still does. There is something of a comfort zone in the manner in which he brings the dying victim back to the area where he is most familiar and most comfortable. There appear to be four dump sites here. The first one is the place in your jurisdiction where the torso was found; the other three sites are less comfortable for him and the dumping occurred at a later date. He lives closer to the first dump site than to the others.

The place where the torso was dumped is interesting for consideration. The residence of this offender is within a close driving distance and perhaps even within vision. The house itself would be nondescript and would blend in with the other

continued

homes in the area. This person is a longtime resident of this community. He would be a person who is well known and probably lived with his mother for a long period, perhaps even to the time of her death.

Vehicle: This person drives a car which is in poor cosmetic condition. The car is 8-10 years old, a domestic car, Ford, Chevrolet, etc., and is also one which is dirty, unkempt, and also in relatively poor mechanical condition. The trunk of the car would also be littered and there would be blood in it which would match the blood of the victim.

Employment: This person is involved in a steady work situation. He is working in some type of construction work and something which demands physical labor. He may also be a truck driver. He is not, however, in a white-collar position. He is involved in a job on a steady basis. He shows some knowledge of the various jurisdictions, and the manner in which the parts were dumped showed some knowledge that police may not always share information. He may at one time have been or presently be a volunteer, an auxiliary police officer, deputy sheriff, medical technician, fireman, etc.

Psychosexual Development: This killer is a seriously disturbed individual. The savagery of the dismemberment depicts someone who has anger directed toward women, appearing in the manner in which he disfigured the face of the victim, i.e., the "smile" on her face. The manner in which he cuts the parts of the body shows determination and anger plus making the victim less than a human being: "Not only are you nothing, now you are little bits of nothing."

The killer has placed the parts is a descending order of preference. First of all, the torso is found days before the other body parts. But with ice particles found in the other parts, this illustrates that he has a lower interest in the torso area, and the other parts are more important since they were kept longer. What is especially interesting is that the person has kept, or at least has not been found, the body from the neck to the waist. This is the most important part for him. I can see him skinning this body part and wearing it at night around the house where he lives alone.

This person may be a transsexual, preoperative one, and may have tried to get counseling for sexual problems. I must stress here that I do not believe he is a homosexual. I think he has a tremendous problem with his sexuality. On the one hand he admires women for who they are, he wants to be like them, and that is the reason he keeps the breasts and looks inside the body cavity at the reproductive organs. But on the other hand, he hates women for the manner in which they (the mother?) have treated him. He also demonstrates this in the manner in which he selects his victims. The victimology shows that this victim was sexually active and frequented lower-class bars, drank excessively, and "ran around on her family." The "victim was deserving" may have been a theme in the fantasy of the killer.

Interrogation: I would be happy to talk with you concerning interrogation strategies when you have effected an arrest.

SOURCE: First author's files.

rapist they believed had committed the majority of the crimes. According to their profile, the offender was white, a high school graduate, of average intelligence, and a loner. This profile proved to be correct, but it was rather limited.

The first author of this volume was also asked to provide a profile in this case. According to that profile, all 34 rapes were committed by one offender, who was white (as described by the victims), married, a Roman Catholic, and employed. He probably lived near where most of the rapes had taken place, and had likely been raised in a sexually repressive home atmosphere. Given that he was Catholic, it was probable that he was not the product of a broken home; that is, it was unlikely that his parents had divorced. He probably now lived in his own home with his wife and children, maybe two or three children, and drove his well-maintained car to the scenes of his rapes.

This profile proved to be remarkably accurate. When the rapist was apprehended, it was found that he was indeed responsible for all the rapes. He was Catholic and lived in his own home with his wife and two children. His parents lived not far from his home, and he worked as a skilled worker for a manufacturing company. He stalked his victims and drove his pickup truck, which was in excellent condition, to the sites of attack.

It would be impressive evidence of the usefulness of profiling if this profile had led directly to the apprehension of this rapist, but this did not prove to be the case. Rather, one of the man's victims happened to recognize him when she saw him later at a shopping center; she followed him to the parking lot and copied down his truck's license number. He was soon arrested, and the case was quickly resolved.

CONCLUSION

The profile developed by Delaney in *The Third Deadly Sin* (Sanders, 1981) illustrates a point we will emphasize again later in this book: The daily activities of police officers provide them with learning opportunities they can put to use in profiling cases. The knowledge base needed for profiling is formed by an understanding of what both physical and nonphysical evidence can reveal and an understanding of basic precepts and principles of the social and behavioral sciences.

The attention to detail in Sherlock Holmes's investigations offers a plain and simple message to police officers: The details, the trifles, are not to be ignored—answers are in the crime scene if one pays attention to them. "There is nothing so important as trifles" (Doyle, 1892, p. 89).

During an interview with the first author, serial killer Ted Bundy said that police officers take their cases too personally. Because of their immersion in their cases, they lose their objectivity. In *The Red Dragon*, Will Graham (Harris, 1981) loses his objectivity, and his total immersion in the crime and into the mind of the killer lead him to emotional and health problems, early retirement, and almost fatal consequences. Of course, profiling in reality is not as neat and precise as it appears to be in fiction, and sometimes profiles go unused. As we have shown, the profile of Hitler developed by Langer was never actually utilized, and the profiles developed in the serial rape case discussed above did not lead directly to apprehension. Some profiles do lead to arrests, however, and we will discuss some of these at length later in this book.

3. Criminal Theories and Psychological Profiling

From the time of Becarria's classical school of criminology in the mid-eighteenth century to the present, humans have made a concentrated effort to focus upon and explain criminal behavior. Many scholars and others have speculated about the exact, single cause of criminality. Free will, positive determinism, genetics, and poverty have all had their time in the spotlight of serious academic examination and debate on this issue.

The behavioral and social sciences have historically examined deviance in general and crime in particular, and both outline basic belief systems that offer insights into the personality of the criminal offender. The primary objective of this chapter is to provide an overview of these basic belief systems. There are sometimes subtle distinctions among theories, and each theoretical system, with its unique perspective and focus, aids in the art of psychological profiling.

PSYCHOLOGY AND THE CRIMINAL PERSONALITY

Belief systems that may be seen as precursors to psychology offered an explanation for crime: demonic possession or evil spirits. As the science of psychology developed, however, the etiology of crime came to be viewed quite differently. Now, as Neitzel (1979) has noted, it is believed that "crime is the result of some personality attribute uniquely possessed, or possessed to a certain degree, by the potential criminal" (p. 350).

Crime is judged psychologically as abnormal. Forensic psychologists, in a quest for the origins of the criminal mind, have paid little attention to individuals' social environments. The search into several research and theoretical areas has continued to identify a single factor as the causal variable for the criminal mind.

MENTAL DEFICIENCY

Early forensic psychologists suggested that crime and delinquency are directly related to mental deficiency or lack of intellectual ability. Deficits in intelligence may have direct influence on social adjustment and may indeed "cause" certain individuals to adopt a criminal or delinquent lifestyle. Studies have indicated that young persons with relatively low IQs may be more prone to delinquency than those with at least average IQ. An IQ, however, is merely a score on a test, and this score can change from one testing session to another. Research of this genre focuses more on the score on a test than on the personality of an offender.

There may be another side to the issue of whether or not IQ is a causal factor in criminal behavior. Individuals with higher intelligence may be more apt to elude capture. It may be that the person with limited mental ability simply lacks the ability to recognize the opportunity to avoid detection and subsequent apprehension, and thus offenders of lower intelligence may be more visible than more intelligent persons in the criminal justice enterprise. However, there are few empirical data available to validate this possibility.

The current modal theoretical position holds that low intelligence has little if anything to do with the development of a criminal mentality.

PERSONALITY CHARACTERISTICS

The particular combination of personality traits necessary to mold a criminal mind is still to be formulated. Research and clinical studies have failed to yield reliable data to confirm any such configuration. Even one of the most often cited tests designed to measure personality traits, the Minnesota Multiphasic Personality Inventory (MMPI), has shown inconsistent results as far as particular personality traits and the criminal mind are concerned (Fisher, 1962).

One study has suggested that delinquent males, compared with nondelinquent males, appear to be more personally aggressive, defiant, hostile, and destructive (Glueck & Glueck, 1950). However, few empirical data are available to substantiate the existence of a criminal or delinquency syndrome.

Dollard et al. (1939) state that the criminal mind has developed a general inability to tolerate frustration without resorting to violence. In our own research, we have found that the very violent lack the ability to withstand frustration. Frustration serves as a catalyst for action, which serves to validate the offender's sense of importance and being in control. As one offender told the first author:

> So when I murdered this first person, it was not to fulfill an inner craving, but only because this person frustrated my aims by being completely unresponsive to my brutality. As this victim was seemingly in a catatonic state, oblivious to my violence, I derived no gain or gratification from my acts, and this individual, therefore, was useless to me.

Obviously, more research needs to be done in this area, but the data thus far do not support any strong indication that any particular combination of personality characteristics combines to produce a criminal mind.

CRIMINAL THINKING PATTERNS

The work of Yochelson and Samenow (1976) suggests that the personality of the criminal is not fundamentally different from that of the noncriminal. In fact, the only difference between the two lies in the criminal's manner of reasoning. Yochelson and Samenow base their theory on interviews with scores of criminals incarcerated in a hospital setting. Although his mentor, Yochelson, places emphasis on the general irresponsibility of the criminal, coupled with his or her erroneous thinking pattern, Samenow (1984) rejects the influence of the environment on the criminal: "It is not the environment that turns a man into a criminal. Rather, it is a series of choices that he makes starting at a very early age" (p. 34). From this perspective, the solution to the problem of crime rests with changing criminals' thought patterns and making it beneficial for them to restructure their perceptions of their world. Only by changing the way criminals think can we change their behavior.

CHARACTER DEFECTS

Psychologists have expended great energy on research into the antisocial personality. Cleckley's *The Mask of Sanity* (1982) is the first major work to describe the behavioral and personality characteristics of individuals with the character defect of psychopathology. According to Cleckley, the psychopath is charming, has no sense of remorse or guilt, is narcissistic, is a habitual liar, has an inadequate sex life, and continually gets into trouble with the law.

There is no single accepted theory regarding what causes psychopathology. It may be that psychopathic individuals have a form of brain damage, and that they tend to come from homes where they have suffered mild rejection. There is less than unanimous agreement that psychopathy actually exists. In his study of hospitalized patients, Cason (1943) found common agreement for only 2 of the 54 behavioral traits supposedly typical of psychopathy. Cason's data suggest that there are no real personality differences between those who exhibit psychopathic behavior and those who do not.

Another possibility posited by some is that psychopathy may indeed be a reality, but that it disappears from the personality by the time a person reaches his or her 30s. This change is theorized based on the argument that the psychopath matures at a much slower rate than most people, reaching maturity around the age of 30. An alternative theory is it that the psychopath adjusts to society, and by his or her 30s is accomplished at masking his or her behavior and thus is able to avoid identification.

Regardless of the various theories concerning the etiology of the criminal mind, psychology offers a perspective unlike any offered by other disciplines. Perhaps most important, methodological psychology offers statistical probabilities regarding demographics as well as behavior and crime.

PSYCHIATRY AND CRIME

Sigmund Freud, the father of the psychodynamic approach to the study of the human mind, devoted little time to the analysis of the human condition and crime. His followers, however, have offered interesting theories regarding the criminal mind. According to Freudian thought, the feelings and behavior of humans arise from a variety of unconscious conflicts among the id, the ego, and the superego. The id is the part of the psyche that represents a human being's biological drives. The superego is the social response component of the psyche; it tells us, "I should want" or "I should not want." The ego is the personality component; it has the task of controlling the savage impulses of the id, which center on sex and aggression. The ego has the mission of controlling and minimizing the conflict between the id and the superego. Crime, in the psychiatric model, is simply symptomatic of these unconscious conflicts. These conflicts, and the resulting overt behaviors, represent a lack of adequate repression of the id or symbolic behavior based on unfulfilled impulses. Criminal behavior is nothing more than behavior that has as its cause unconscious dynamics, of which the criminal ordinarily has little or no understanding. As Abrahamsen (1944) notes, "The criminal rarely knows completely the reasons for his conduct" (p. 21).

The criminal may have either an overdeveloped or an underdeveloped superego. Whichever is the case, this leads to a psychological state of guilt and anxiety, or *anomie*. Because of this feeling of anomie, the individual is in a constant state of desire for punishment—punishment that will remove the guilt and anxiety and will restore the person to a state of psychological equilibrium.

The source of trauma to the superego originates in early childhood. The unregulated id is the direct link to crime, but, because of early conflict, the guilt is evident in youth. Freud (1948) was aware of this:

> In many criminals, especially youthful ones, it is possible to detect a very powerful sense of guilt which existed before the crime, and is therefore not its result but its motive. It is as if it was a relief to be able to fasten the unconscious sense of guilt onto something real and immediate. (p. 52)

A major criticism leveled against psychiatry in general is its resistance to empirical testing. Obviously, the existence of the id, the ego, and the superego, and their relationship to crime, has never been empirically verified. This is not to say that serious research has not been attempted. Aichorn (1935), for example, has related an underdeveloped superego to the criminal personality. Abrahamsen (1944, p. 137) views the criminal as an id-dominated person. That is, the criminal responds to the basic aggressive and sexual urges of the id and fails to evaluate or appreciate the pain and suffering of the victim.

In summary, the psychiatric approach to the criminal personality focuses on the role of sex and aggression and on means of adaptation learned during early childhood. Its main contribution to criminal theory is the creation of an awareness of the unconscious and the role of guilt and anxiety as they relate to crime.

SOCIAL THEORIES AND CRIME

Social theorists are concerned with the etiology of criminal behavior as it interacts with society's social structures and processes. Their focus tends to be on norm violation and social definitions of deviance.

According to the structural/functionalist perspective on deviance and crime, society attempts to function as a well-oiled, integrated, and orderly machine. Ideally, citizens would unanimously agree upon the society's values and goals, and social structures would function to implement these values and goals. Deviance and crime represent breakdowns in this social consensus.

The structural/functionalist approach can be traced to the writings of Emile Durkheim (1965), who suggested that different interest groups have varied and conflicting views about right and wrong. Durkheim's main contribution rests in his emphasis on the organization of social life rather than on psychological causes. He originated his theory of crime in the context of a movement toward modernization, the progression of a society from the organic to the mechanistic. The high rate of crime in mechanistic societies rests with the general feeling of anomie, a feeling of helplessness or normlessness.

Other sociologists have addressed the strain between society and the individual. Robert Merton (1968), for example, offers a theory that maintains that both social ends and the means to achieve those ends are learned. Some people in a society will have high aspirations; some will not. In U.S. society, economic rewards are deemed to be a socially approved goal. Many people, however, are societally blocked from reaching that goal—the cultural goal exceeds the structural opportunities. Crime may result from such a situation through the adaptation to anomie that Merton terms "innovation." The criminal will resort to illegitimate means to attain legitimate goals, such as a "nice" home in a middle-class residential area where the crime rate is low.

THE CHICAGO SCHOOL

In the 1930s, an important sociological perspective developed among a group of scholars at the University of Chicago. Important theoreticians such as Burgess, Reckless, Dinitz, Glaser, and Sutherland all became well-known names associated with this social ecological approach.

Edwin Sutherland's (1937) theory of differential association is more than a cultural transmission theory. According to Sutherland, criminal behavior is learned in primary group relationships, not through exposure to mass media, such as television, movies, radio, and comic books. This is not to say that some techniques for committing crimes may not be learned from these sources, but the inculcation of the necessary motives, drives, direction, and rationalization for the commission of crime takes place on a conscious level. The rearing of an individual with a criminal mind-set rests upon the person's affiliation with those who favor violation of the law and those who favor obeying the law.

Perhaps the most recent influential theory of deviance has been offered by Travis Hirschi (1969), who asserts that there is a bond between people and conventional society. There are several basic elements in the theoretical construct of norms of a society that are internalized. *Attachment* refers to a person's sensitivity to the way people think about him or her. *Commitment* is the extent to which a person's social rewards are connected to social conformity. Finally, *involvement* refers to the amount of time a societal member devotes to conventional activity. The higher the level of involvement, the lower the probability of criminal activity.

In essence, social theorists have taken the position that the criminal has learned to or has been compelled to commit crime by social situations. The core of the criminal commitment lies within the personality of the offender and the fiber of the society. The society contains the goals, both legitimate and illegitimate means, objectives, and opportunities, as well as proscriptions concerning criminal behavior. Sociologists place little emphasis on the role of the

unconscious in deviance, or on mental deficiency as a causal deter-
minant in crime.

COMBINING THE DISCIPLINES

Clearly, each of the disciplines discussed above has a distinct
focus and direction for understanding the mind of the criminal. It
may well be that the psychopath, properly understood, appears more
often in certain categories in society, and this can be better explained
from a sociological perspective than from a psychiatric or psychological one. If a person is a loner because of mental deficiency,
personal choice, or some socially defined "weirdness," a blend of
the disciplines of psychology and psychiatry may give the profiler
an understanding of such an individual's personality. Sociology can
aid the profiler in developing an understanding of the network of
personal, social, occupational, and support relationships that such a
personal will develop.

The value of the various theories that come from these disciplines
is found in the profiler's ability to blend them to reach an understanding of the personality of the perpetrator. There is nothing
magical or mystical about this process; its success depends on the
"truths" of the disciplines and how they add to the knowledge base
of the law enforcement professional. Academic theories will never
take the place of on-the-street police work, and the psychological
profile is not intended to bolster or refute academic theory; it is
simply another tool available for use in the total investigative
process.

4. The Rationale for Psychological Profiling

Whenever a particularly bizarre and sadistic crime is discovered, an immediate question comes to mind: What kind of a person would commit such an act? Most such crimes defy understanding and leave us with a sense of bewilderment and astonishment. The real question, however, is, What makes someone do something like this? What composes a personality who enjoys mutilation, necrophilia, rape, or other forms of perversion and pain? To address such questions, profiling constructs personality sketches for evaluation.

PERSONALITY AND CRIME

In meeting the challenge of apprehending and successfully prosecuting the perpetrators of such crimes as sexual torture, rape, and child molestation, personality profiling can be an invaluable tool. Personality profilers endeavor to shed some light on the types of persons who rape, mutilate, and kill. A personality is nothing more than the sum total of what a person is. It is that person's total set of values and attitudes: the way he or she views motherhood and fatherhood, law and order, Democrats and Republicans, and all the other social, cultural, religious, and personal experiences that have been a part of his or her life.

Each human being has a unique personality. Regardless of past experiences, parental background, and biology, each person has a unique way of relating to others, a unique way of behaving, and a unique set of values and attitudes. Five basic components—biology, culture, environment, common experiences, and unique experiences— combine to make up the personality of each individual person, so that no two persons are exactly alike.

BIOLOGY

There are no data suggesting that an individual's personality is determined *solely* by biological inheritance. It does appear that people of superior intelligence tend to have children who are also of superior intelligence. It is also true that tall people tend to have tall children, and short people tend to have short children, but, of course, there are always exceptions. As far as intelligence is concerned, some children may score higher on standardized tests because of social factors (such as their parents' education, membership in a privileged class, and respect and encouragement for learning in the home), and not simply because of biological inheritance.

CULTURE

The culture in which a person is reared provides him or her with norms and values. The culture—the normative structure of a society, with the prevailing words, ideas, customs, and beliefs of the power- ful persons who live in the society—instructs the individual in the "proper" way to behave.

Within each culture, however, there are subcultures: male and female, poor and rich, criminal and noncriminal, and so on. These subcultures have certain distinguishable characteristics that set them apart from the overall, prevailing culture. Each subculture insists upon certain patterns of behavior and rewards its members in unique fashion. In other words, a person brought up in one part of a society will be exposed to elements of that society that are different from those found in other parts of the society. This exposure will have an influence on personality development.

ENVIRONMENT

The surroundings in which a person lives will affect his or her perceptions and behavior. A person from the upper class, for example, is exposed to a far different set of life experiences than is a person from the lower class. A person's day-to-day experiences become an integral part of his or her personality, and social class status has great influence on the range of experiences—as well as opportunities—with which an individual comes in contact.

COMMON EXPERIENCES

Within a society, there are many experiences that are common to all or almost all of the society's members. In the United States, most of us have had contact with some form of school system, with baseball and other sports, with automobiles, with marriage and divorce, and so on. In contrast, all of us have not been to the same school, or been taught by the same teachers. Not all of us have been reared by the same parents, and not all of our parents are happily married. Not all children are brought up by their biological parents—some are reared by their grandparents, by foster parents, or by others. In spite of our differences, Americans have developed what may be considered a modal personality type that encompasses certain ideals: trustworthiness, loyalty, honesty, reverence, and other values that most of us hold dear.

UNIQUE EXPERIENCES

What separates individuals from one another are not their common experiences but their unique ones. A great deal of what accounts for personality differences among individuals lies in their personal and unique experiences. Consider identical twins, who have the same biological inheritance and usually the same environment, at least in childhood, yet often have marked personality differences. The unique events of twins' daily lives from the time they are born—the differing sequences of feedings, diaper changes, and other attention from adults—must account, at least in part, for differences in their personalities.

NEW WAYS OF VIEWING THE PERSONALITY

The personality of the violent offender is far different from that of most individuals in the same society; such an individual does not share in the values held as part of American society's modal personality type. Many theorists have attempted to explain why these individuals are so different, but no satisfactory explanation has been found. Because the very violent do not share in the values of the society, and because impersonal violence is so difficult to understand, it is often assumed that the perpetrators of violence reflect a pathological personality condition. This pathology is reflected in their crime scenes.

This is really not an extraordinary assumption; similar comments could be made about law-abiding but neurotic persons. Social and behavioral scientists have long known that a person's surroundings reflect his or her personality. In the case of an obsessive-compulsive person, for example, the compulsion is evident in the individual's home, car, personal effects, and personal hygiene. This personality disorder takes over the person's daily life activities. So it is with the very violent—their personality traits are reflected in the ways they perpetrate their crimes. If one accepts this premise, then the viewing of crime scenes takes on a totally new perspective. This will be useful, however, only if the profiler knows what to look for and where to look for it.

ASSUMPTIONS OF THE PROFILING PROCESS

THE CRIME SCENE REFLECTS THE PERSONALITY

The basic assumption of psychological profiling is that the crime scene reflects the personality of the offender. Thus, assessment of the crime scene should aid police by providing direction for their investigation of the crime, including the narrowing of the scope of the investigation.

The manner in which a victim has been killed is very important, but other physical and nonphysical evidence also can be very valuable in the assessment of the murderer's personality. The amount of chaos at the scene, for example, might indicate that a disorganized personality was involved in the crime. If this is true, then certain assumptions can be made about the social core variables of the perpetrator (see Chapter 5 for further discussion of disorganized and organized offenders). On the other hand, if the crime scene is "neat and clean," or if the murder appears to be a "five window killing" (discussed in Chapter 6), then other assumptions might lead to an offender with a different set of social core variables.

The focus of the attack may also indicate certain information that can aid in the apprehension of an unknown offender. An example of a case in which this was true is one in which an elderly woman was killed in her own home in a midwestern state. She was stabbed repeatedly and suffered multiple deep wounds to the upper legs and genital area. For reasons that we will address in a later chapter, the profile offered an assessment of the crime that, in part, resulted in the arrest of the killer, a man who was not considered a suspect at the beginning stages of the law enforcement investigation.

The profiler must take into account the total crime scene in order to form a mental image of the personality of the offender.

> I had once read a pornography book in my father's garage. This book was about rape. I believe I memorized the whole book. There was one part of the book which described a rape of a young girl. I made all of the girls I raped repeat the words of the girl in the book. This was the only way I could enjoy the rapes. Eventually, it was not enough to rape. The girl in the book was killed. I had to kill. (first author's files)

The killer who made this statement learned from an experience with violent pornography. In addition, because of a constellation of other elements—his family background, his social and biological inheritance, and his life experiences—he gained sexual pleasure and personal satisfaction from the rapes and killings of scores of women. This killer was unable to stop raping and killing as long as he was physically free to do so. The urge became similar to an addiction.

> There is no denying that once the cycle of violence is set into motion, violence itself becomes a habit, a need which must be sated repeatedly thereafter. And, in this general sense, I'm sure it can be said that [the offender] is addicted to impersonal violence. (first author's files)

The urge, compulsion, or addiction became part of the killer's personality. The manifestation of the urge became part of each of his crimes. Again and again, he acted out the scenario in his father's pornography.

THE METHOD OF OPERATION REMAINS SIMILAR

It is the behavior of the perpetrator, as evidenced in the crime scene, and not the offense per se, that determines the degree of suitability of a case for profiling (Geberth, 1993, p. 401). The crime scene contains clues that an experienced profiler may determine to be the "signature" of a criminal. Just as no two offenders are exactly alike, it is equally true that no two crime scenes are exactly alike. As certainly as a psychometric test reflects psychopathology, the crime scene reflects a personality with a pathology.

Many serial offenders themselves are quite aware of the non-physical evidence present at a crime scene. One murderer remarked:

First of all, any investigative onlooker to my crime scene would have immediately deduced that the offender was extremely sadistic in nature. The visible markers of bondage, and the nature of the victims' wounds—the evidence of unhurried, systematic abuse—would have indicated that sadistic acts were not new to the offender; he had committed such brutality in the past, and would likely continue this pattern of victimization in the future.

From these points, it could have then been correctly assumed that, although brutally violent, the offender was nevertheless intelligent enough to attach method to his madness—as well as cautious and aware enough with regard to his surroundings—to make sure he proceeds unseen in the commission of his deeds.

Further, . . . such a brutal offense was unprecedented in this area, it could have been correctly assumed that the offender was very new to the city; if he was a drifter, he was at least someone who very possibly could deem to leave town as suddenly as he arrived (which is exactly what I did). (first author's files)

This killer's remarks show the one dimension of personality, the conscious dimension, that profiling often neglects. This murderer and rapist illustrates by his remarks the elements within his crime scenes that truly reflected his personality. He repeated this MO many times in the course of his rapes and murders.

The infamous Boston Strangler also had a typical MO, as the following illustrates:

Case study: From June 1961 to the following January, Boston was terrorized by the brutal murders and strangulations of 13 women. The crime scenes reflected hate, chaos, and other elements that serve as the impetus for profiling. For example, Mary Sullivan, Albert De-Salvo's last victim, was found nude in her bed. A broom handle was found inserted into her vagina, both breasts were exposed, and the Boston Strangler had ejaculated onto her face and into her mouth.

A profiling committee, composed of a psychiatrist, a gynecologist, an anthropologist, and others, was established, and a "psychiatric profile" was developed. The committee suspected two offenders in the 13 killings. According to the committee's profile, one killer, Mr. S., was "raised by a domineering seductive mother; unable to express hatred toward his mother and directing instead the anger toward other women, especially older women; lived alone, and once he was able to conquer his domineering mother, he could love like normal people." The committee believed that the younger victims had been killed by a homosexual who was acquainted with the victims.

Albert DeSalvo was eventually apprehended and convicted, not as the Boston Strangler, but on a property charge. DeSalvo, married and living with his wife, had an insatiable sexual appetite. He demanded sex from his wife five or six times a day. He was sentenced to life in prison for the crimes of the "Green Man." After only a few days in prison, DeSalvo escaped, but he was quickly reapprehended. For the next few years, he served his sentence without incident, until he was stabbed to death by another inmate. (Frank, 1966, p. 379)

THE SIGNATURE WILL REMAIN THE SAME

The *signature* of a perpetrator is the unique manner in which he or she commits crimes. A signature may be the manner in which the person kills, certain words a rapist uses with victims, a particular manner in which a perpetrator leaves something at crime scenes, or some other indicator.

The following case illustrates the nature of one killer's signature. In a midwestern state, two elderly women were murdered. Neither was raped, and both were left in a public park in full view. On their stomachs were placed their driver's licenses and their keys. In another state, several hundred miles away, a female impersonator was killed in a similar fashion, strangled, and his driver's license and his keys were also left on his stomach. At first, it appeared that there were two killers, because the victims were different: two elderly females and one young man who was allegedly homosexual and a drag queen. The victimology would not suggest that these crimes were committed by the same person. However, the signature, the placement of the victim's driver's license and keys, was the same in all three cases. This signature should have alerted investigators that the crimes were committed by the same person; cooperation between the various jurisdictions in which the crimes took place could have facilitated the investigation.

Ray Hazelwood, a retired FBI agent who spent the latter part of his career with the Bureau's Behavioral Science Unit, now delivers lectures to law enforcement groups across the United States about the importance of considering the offender's signature and its influence on the profiling process (e.g., Hazelwood, 1994).

THE OFFENDER'S PERSONALITY WILL NOT CHANGE

It is generally agreed that the core of a person's personality does not change fundamentally over time. A person may change certain aspects of him- or herself, but the central elements of the personality are set, and only minor alterations may be made due to time, circumstance, pressure, and so on. Even when a person wants to make fundamental personality changes, he or she will find that it is difficult or even impossible to do so.

So it is with the criminal personality. Offenders have taken years to become the persons they are, and they will not, over a short period, radically change. It is not simply a matter of not wanting to change—they are not able to change even if they want to. This assumption has fundamental importance to the profiling process. The offender's inability to change results in the perpetration of similar crimes in similar fashion. The criminal may not only commit the same crime, but may force each victim to act out a scenario that previous victims have been forced to perform.

THE WORTH OF THE PSYCHOLOGICAL PROFILE

Not all profiles are as inaccurate as the one that was constructed in the Boston Strangler case. Perhaps one of the most accurate ever developed was the one Dr. James Brussel, a psychiatrist, created concerning the "Mad Bomber," George Metesky. Brussel accurately predicted that when the Bomber was eventually caught, he would be wearing a double-breasted suit. Amazingly, this was true.

Despite the accuracy of this particular profile, some critics believe that profiling has still not proven its worth. Godwin (1978) asserts:

> Nine out of ten of the profiles are vapid. They play at blind man's bluff, groping in all directions in the hope of touching a sleeve. Occasionally they do, but not firmly enough to seize it, for the behaviorists producing them must necessarily deal in generalities and types. But policemen can't arrest a type. They require hard data: names, dates, none of which the psychiatrists can offer. (p. 202)

Even the Federal Bureau of Investigation's research on the reliability and validity of profiling shows less than unanimous endorsement of the profiling process. In a study of 192 cases where profiling was performed, 88 cases were solved. Of those 88, in only 17% did a profile help in the identification of a suspect. The Bureau has noted, however, that its profile in the Wayne Williams case helped "break [Williams's] composure on the witness stand" (Porter, 1983). This claim has been hotly contested, however, by Chet Dettlinger, a member of Williams's defense team. His contention, supported by Dr. Robert E. Blackwelder (personal communication, March 10, 1987), another member of the defense team, is that the defense attorney wanted the jurors to see the "real Wayne Williams" on the stand, a gamble that backfired (Dettlinger & Prugh, 1984).

Jenkins (1994, pp. 70-79) has leveled a scathing attack on the worth of the profiles offered by FBI agents Douglas, Ressler, and Hazelwood. Jenkins cites Ganey's (1989, p. 22) observation that Hazelwood, now retired, offered the most "inaccurate profile in the Bureau's history" in the Charlie Hatcher case. Another debacle was the Clayton Hartwig profile, concerning the explosion aboard the U.S. battleship *Iowa* (Jeffers, 1992, pp. 177-229; cited in Jenkins, 1994). Jenkins (1994, p. 71) also says that Paul Lindsey, a former special agent with the FBI, has denounced the claims made by Ressler in his autobiography *Whoever Fights Monsters* (Ressler & Shachtman, 1992). In addition, Jenkins cites Smith and Guillen (1990), who have written about a case for which Douglas was brought in to offer a profile—a case that is still unsolved 10 years after the crime.

Despite the claims of the FBI concerning the validity of its profiles and huge resources available to the Bureau, there is less than total agreement among those in law enforcement that profiles—specifically from the Bureau or generally from others—constitute a key element in the investigatory process. Regardless, profiling continues to be a part of many investigatory efforts.

CONCLUSION

The personality of the violent offender is a result of a special combination of factors, including biological inheritance, culture, environment, and common and unique experiences. Because of this unique combination, the violent personal offender will commit crimes as an outgrowth of existing pathological conditions.

The crime scene reflects the pathology of the offender's personality. Nonphysical evidence as well as physical evidence can have important ramifications for the psychological profiling process. Because the personalities of individuals, both noncriminal and criminal, are relatively inflexible, offenders tend to commit the same or similar crimes utilizing the same or similar MOs.

The inflexibility of personality and its influence on the perpetration of crimes aid the profiler in the task of developing a character sketch. Chaos or order, sexual torture or a quick kill, mutilation or not—each indicates a personality that has evolved over the years. It is no easier for a person with a violent personality to change suddenly and completely than it is for a law-abiding citizen.

5. The Analysis of the Crime Scene

Obviously, some crimes are more appropriate for profiling than others. We have listed these crimes in Chapter 1: sadistic torture in sexual assault, evisceration, postmortem slashing and cutting, motiveless fire setting, lust and mutilation murder, and rape (stranger rape, not date or acquaintance rape). Such crimes as check forgery, bank robbery, and kidnapping, in contrast, are usually not appropriate candidates for profiling, nor are "smoking gun" or "dripping knife" murders. In this chapter we focus on those crimes to which the process of profiling is directly applicable.

BEYOND THE PHYSICAL EVIDENCE

Perhaps one of the most difficult things for investigators to accept is the need to look beyond the physical evidence. Homicide detectives are generally trained to reconstruct a crime based on the physical evidence found at the scene, such as blood spatters, fingerprints, and semen. This kind of evidence is often mistakenly thought to hold the key to the successful resolution of *any* criminal case.

Recently, the first author lectured on psychological profiling at the Southern Police Institute. In reviewing the basic elements of the profiling process, he used several resolved and unresolved cases as case studies. The cases in which profiling led to a narrowing of the field of suspects and to an ultimate arrest contained nonphysical evidence from which a profiler could deduce useful information about a suspect: race, sex, employment status, residence, and so on. Despite the author's several admonitions to the students to disregard the physical evidence and concentrate on nonphysical factors, the students were reluctant to do so. Only after repeated urging were they able to examine the nonphysical evidence. The physical evidence was then reintroduced, and the crime reconstructed. It is the interrelationship of physical evidence and nonphysical evidence that is the key to the profiling process.

A PSYCHOLOGICAL PROFILING TYPOLOGY

The Federal Bureau of Investigation has developed a typology of lust offenders that many profilers find particularly useful; it divides offenders into two categories—*disorganized asocial* offenders and *organized nonsocial* offenders. In their book *Sexual Homicide,* Ressler, Burgess, and Douglas (1988) delete the labels *asocial* and *nonsocial* in describing this typology. We believe this is unfortunate, because the descriptive nature of these words is useful. There is a fundamental difference between nonsocial and asocial behaviors, and these adjectives add valuable information that can help clarify the differences between organized and disorganized offenders. For the purposes of this text, we use the full original label to identify each type of offender.[1]

This typology can be useful when the crimes at issue involve sex as a primary motive. The offenders who commit such crimes as rape, sexual assault, mutilation, necrophilia, and picquerism are particularly amenable to categorization as organized nonsocial or disorganized asocial offenders.

TABLE 5.1 Profile Characteristics of Disorganized Asocial Offenders

Personal Characteristics	Postoffense Behavior	Interview Techniques
Below-average intelligence	Returns to crime scene	Show empathy
Socially inadequate	May attend victim's	Introduce information
Unskilled worker	funeral/burial	indirectly
Low birth-order status	May place "in memoriam"	Use counselor approach
Father's work unstable	messages in media	Interview at night
Received harsh/inconsistent	May turn to religion	
discipline in childhood	May keep diary or news	
Anxious mood during crime	clippings	
Minimal use of alcohol	May change residence	
Lives alone	May change job	
Lives/works near crime	May have a personality change	
scene		
Minimal interest in news		
media		
Significant behavioral		
change		
Nocturnal		
Poor personal hygiene		
Secret hiding places		
Usually does not date		
High school dropout		

SOURCE: "Crime Scene" (1985).

THE DISORGANIZED ASOCIAL OFFENDER

Personal characteristics. As the list of characteristics in Table 5.1 shows, the personality of this kind of offender is reflected in the label. The disorganized asocial offender, who is almost always male, is disorganized in his daily activities as well as in his general surroundings, including home, employment (if he is employed), car or truck, clothing, and demeanor. In other words, he is a totally disorganized person in all areas—appearance, lifestyle, and psychological state. We should note that this is a general description, and it has not been empirically validated. Nonetheless, in the cases where a "pure" such personality has been found, these general characteristics have proven to be amazingly accurate.

According to the FBI's research data, the typical offender with a disorganized asocial personality tends to be a nonathletic, introverted white male. As children, many of these offenders have been victims of physical or emotional abuse. Their fathers were often absent; if the fathers were present and employed, their work was unstable. During their childhoods, these offenders had few real playmates; they tended to have solitary hobbies, to have imaginary and secret playmates, and to take part in few social activities. The disorganized asocial offender is a loner. The reason for this aloneness, however, is fundamentally different from that behind the aloneness of the organized nonsocial offender. The disorganized asocial offender is a loner because he is perceived by others to be "weird" or strange—his neighbors are often aware of his strangeness.

This perpetrator has usually experienced a great deal of difficulty in educational pursuits. While in high school, he participated little in extracurricular activities, and he probably dropped out of school as soon as legally possible. He is possibly below average in IQ (the FBI estimates the IQ of the typical disorganized asocial offender to be between 80 and 95), but this may be more a product of his social and cultural experiences than his native intelligence.

His status in his community is the product of several components of his personality. Limited intelligence, involvement in unskilled work (often as a menial laborer), and few dates or other social contacts with women—all reflect a person who is alone not by choice but because of societal segregation.

Because of the combination of components described above, the disorganized asocial offender lacks the ability to plan out his crimes efficiently, and the crimes tend to be spontaneous acts. This kind of offender does not feel comfortable venturing far from his home or work, so he often commits crimes in his own neighborhood. He may walk or ride a bicycle to his crime sites ("Crime Scene," 1985). Generally, this kind of offender does not feel the need to follow his crimes in the news media.

The disorganized asocial offender normally lacks the initiative to practice good personal hygiene. This same characteristic carries over to his domicile, as well as to any car or truck he may own. This trait, then, may theoretically carry over into the crime scene. Finally, as with all lust offenders, he will repeat his crimes.

Postoffense behavior. According to the researchers at the Behavioral Science Unit (BSU) of the FBI, the disorganized asocial offender will tend to exhibit certain behavior patterns after he has committed a crime. First, he will need to return to the scene of the crime relatively soon afterward, to envision and relive what has taken place. He may attend the funeral services of his victim, even the burial ceremony. It is not unheard of for such an offender to place an "in memoriam" message in the newspaper for his victim.

This offender may keep a diary in which he records his activities and victims. With the current widespread availability of instant photography and videotape equipment, it may be that soon this type of violent personal offender will commonly keep pictorial representations of his crimes. A part of this type of offender's diary, in addition to accounts of his acts, may be devoted to stories of his fantasies. One serial rapist related the following fantasy:

> My preference is for tight teenage girls—the tighter the better.
> [Talking with another rapist] We've got to do this the *right* way. You really blew it but you were inexperienced. The first thing is to get a house with a windowless, underground basement. Equip it with steel cages [for holding victims], and make sure to soundproof it. Only then will we go out and hunt.
> But not just for anyone. Take your time, and find exactly what you want—you don't want to be attracting attention by snatching up a new one every little while. Find one that's perfect. Then we'll keep her locked up before you kill her and grab another. But if we torture, we'd best grab two so that we will always have one recovering while we're busy on the other. (first author's files)

After an offense, the disorganized asocial offender may change his address, but it would be unusual for him to move to a far different environment, because he feels comfortable only with the familiar. If he moves to an area that is drastically different, he may suffer great feelings of anomie. He may therefore move to a similar domicile in a similar area. He may even change jobs. Some may try to enlist in the military, but this is usually unsuccessful, because they either cannot pass the physical or psychological tests or, once enlisted, receive a general discharge.

Interviewing techniques. Once in custody, the disorganized asocial offender may respond differently to questioning than may the organized nonsocial offender. This perpetrator may be more likely to respond to an interrogator who uses a relationship-motivated strategy. It may be a good idea for the interrogator to appear to empathize with him. For example, if an offender says that he has seen a demon and that the demon demanded that he kill, it might be wise for his questioner to tell him that although the questioner has not personally seen this demon, if the killer says it exists, it does indeed exist.

Because this kind of offender is not used to lengthy personal contacts with others, it may be beneficial for interrogators to keep up a constant stream of conversation, perhaps introducing something into the conversation that has to do with the crime scene. The establishment of a positive personal relationship may also prove beneficial in securing some statement concerning the involvement of the suspect in the case.

Another characteristic of the disorganized asocial offender that may be useful for interrogators to know is that he tends to be a night person. Considering this, the interviewer might take the opportunity to interview this person when he is at "his best"—at night.

THE ORGANIZED NONSOCIAL OFFENDER

Personal characteristics. The organized nonsocial offender is the disorganized asocial offender's opposite. He has an organized personality that is reflected in his lifestyle, home, automobile, and personal appearance.[2] This kind of offender may be called an anal personality type; in his life, there is a place for everything and everything must be in its place.

Ted Bundy is an example of such an offender. Because of his personality, Bundy would have found it very difficult to deviate from his accustomed way of doing things. As a result, he was connected with at least four murders because he charged his gasoline and signed receipts for his purchases. He was placed in Golden, Colorado, on the day Suzy Cooley was abducted and killed; in Dillon, Colorado, when Julie Cunningham was murdered; and in Grand

TABLE 5.2 Profile Characteristics of the Organized Nonsocial Offender

Personal Characteristics	Postoffense Behavior	Interview Techniques
High intelligence	Returns to crime scene	Use direct strategy
Socially adequate	Volunteers information	Be certain of details
Sexually competent	Police groupie	Be aware that offender will
Lives with partner	Anticipates questioning	admit to only what he must
High birth order	May move body	
Harsh discipline in childhood	May dispose of body to	
Controlled mood	advertise crime	
Masculine image		
Charming		
Situational cause		
Geographically mobile		
Occupationally mobile		
Follows media		
Model prisoner		

SOURCE: "Crime Scene" (1985).

Junction, Colorado, when Denise Oliverson was reported missing. Michael Fisher was able to secure a murder indictment against Bundy in the Caryn Campbell case when Fisher was able to place Bundy in the immediate vicinity of the Snowmass Ski Lodge because of his gasoline purchases.

As Table 5.2 shows, organized nonsocial offenders are basically organized in everything they do. They are nonsocial because they choose to be so. These offenders' solitariness is different from that of disorganized asocial offenders, who, as noted above, are loners because they appear to be strange. Organized nonsocial offenders are loners because they often feel that no one else is good enough to be around them.

In addition, there are precipitating factors involved in the crimes of the organized nonsocial personality ("Crime Scene," 1985, p. 19). These precipitating factors may be either real or imagined. As one serial killer told the first author:

> One night I finally got a date with a young woman I had been trying to date for 6 months. We went out for a drink before dinner. We were sitting at the bar when a guy walked by. She watched him as he

walked down the bar. I felt that she should not look at him while she was with me. So, what could I do? I killed her.

The young woman who was this killer's victim had challenged his sense of self-importance. The killer believed he "had no choice"— he had to kill to regain his rightful position. Although the damage this offender perceived the woman had done him was only imagined, it was enough.

Other attributes of the organized offender include average intelligence; some such offenders may have done well in school, and many are at least high school graduates. (Ted Bundy was a college graduate and a law school student.) These offenders are socially competent and have sex partners. Some are married, and most are intimate with someone. Many come from middle-class families and are high in the birth order. Their fathers held stable jobs and were often inconsistent about discipline. For many such offenders there is a history of some drug use, especially alcohol and marijuana. Bundy, again as an example, was a heavy user of alcohol and marijuana during his crimes.

The organized offender feels comfortable venturing away from his home. He is able to work and carry on personal, although superficial, relationships. He also is psychologically able to widen his network of relationships and can travel farther and farther away from his home and work to cruise for victims, and, more important, to hinder his apprehension.

Because of his personality, this type of offender has no trouble making friends. He is also able to change employment as often as he chooses because he makes such a good impression and appears to have qualifications that he may in reality not possess. Many have good positions. John Gacy owned a construction company. Chris Wilder was a race car driver. Ken Bianchi was a "psychologist" and security officer.

The organized nonsocial offender has a masculine personality. He often dresses in a flashy manner and drives a car that reflects his personality. As mentioned above, unlike the disorganized asocial personality offender, he feels comfortable in widening his range when cruising for victims, or when trying to avoid detection. Using Bundy again as a prime example, he was suspected of abducting Roberta Kathy Parks from the campus of Oregon State University. He drove her (apparently still alive) almost 300 miles back to Seattle. This was not an isolated incident. He also was alleged to have driven from Seattle to Ellensburg, Washington, for the abduction and murder of Susan Rancourt. The disorganized offender, in contrast, ranges only within his immediate neighborhood, because this is the only place he feels comfortable.

With a positive self-image bordering on egomania, the organized nonsocial offender may be said to have a character disorder. Commonly, he is termed a full-blown sociopath. He believes that he knows best, not only for himself but for everyone else as well. Because he is always right, he is reluctant to accept criticism, even when it is meant constructively; this offender perceives any kind of criticism to be destructive.

Postoffense behavior. For the organized nonsocial offender, the crime becomes—at least partially—a game. Such an offender will often return to the scene of the crime for the purpose of reliving the sensations he felt there. Some, like Edmund Kemper, will be tempted to return to the scene but will not because they have "seen one too many stories of one too many people" who have been caught by the police when they did so—a piece of information Kemper picked up from watching television. The organized nonsocial offender often learns many details of police work from television and other sources. He may even associate with police or other law enforcement agencies, because the police talk about the cases that are special to them. As Kemper said of his relationships with police, "I became a friendly nuisance" (Home Box Office, 1984).

In interviewing one serial killer, the first author mentioned to him that although the man was suspected of killing scores of young women, only a few of the bodies had ever been found. The killer's reaction was, "You only find the bodies they [the serial killers] want you to find." When asked why a killer would want some bodies to be found and not others, he said, "To let you know he's still there."

Because of his charm and charismatic personality, this person may be the last to be suspected of a crime. Even if suspected, because he often possesses intelligence and social graces, he may be able to anticipate investigators' questions and prepare responses to suit his own situation.

Interviewing techniques. The BSU recommends that this kind of offender be confronted directly during the interviewing session. Offenders of this type respect competence, even when it may lead to their arrest and conviction. However, when using such confrontation in the interrogation, the interviewer must be absolutely confident about his or her information. If the interviewer presents "the facts," he or she must be certain that they are true and accurate. This type of offender will know immediately when he is being conned, and he will understand immediately if false "evidence" is presented to him that the police actually have no case. This can close the door on successful resolution of a case, because the offender will never volunteer any information that can be taken as any kind of admission of guilt. This type of offender will admit to only what he must. The interrogator should not hope that once he is confronted with all the known facts the floodgates of information will open.

Some believe that a single-interviewer strategy is best. In the Ted Bundy case, Donald Patchen and Steven Bodiford (1978) interrogated Bundy frequently during a short period. The interviews took place mostly at night. Finally, after several sessions, Bundy admitted, "There's something deep inside me, something I can't control." However, after he had the chance to sleep and psychologically regroup, Bundy denied having admitted even that.

CRIME SCENE DIFFERENCES

It has been theorized that the crime scenes of organized nonsocial offenders and disorganized asocial offenders will differ along the same lines as the differences in their personalities (see Table 5.3). That is, those who are organized in their lives in general will also

TABLE 5.3 Comparison of Crime Scenes of Organized Nonsocial and Disorganized Asocial Lust Killers

Organized Nonsocial Killer	Disorganized Asocial Killer
Planned offense	Spontaneous event
Targeted stranger	Victim unknown
Personalizes victim	Depersonalizes victim
Controlled conversation	Minimal conversation
Controlled crime scene	Chaotic crime scene
Submissive victim	Sudden violence
Restraints used	No restraints
Aggressive acts	Sex after death
Body moved	Body not moved
Weapon taken	Weapon left
Little evidence	Physical evidence

SOURCE: "Crime Scene" (1985).

be organized in the perpetration of their crimes, and those who are disorganized in their everyday lives will be disorganized in the perpetration of their crimes, and so differing degrees of organization and disorganization should be evident in crime scenes.

The organized nonsocial offender takes great care in the perpetration of his violence. This offender makes certain that the evidence will be destroyed. Also, in the case of homicide, he will often kill at one site and dispose of the body at another site. The disorganized offender, on the other hand, attacks his victims suddenly, in unplanned or barely planned violence. The surprise, or blitz, attack results in a crime scene that holds a great deal of physical evidence. The following case provides an example.

Case study: A 75-year-old widow had lived in the same housing project since 1937 and had been living alone since the mid-1960s. On July 4, when her son came to pick her up to spend the holiday with his family, he found his mother's body in her bed. She had been stabbed repeatedly and decapitated. The weapon was a butcher knife that had belonged to the victim. Blood spatter was found on the walls by her bed as well as on the ceiling, showing that the attack had been carried out in a frenzy. The woman had been sexually assaulted, and semen was found in her vaginal vault as well as on the bedspread and in the bedclothes.

There was a great deal of physical evidence at the scene. No other murders similar to this one were known, and a profile was requested. The profile suggested that the offender was a black male, early 20s, single, living within the immediate neighborhood, and living with his mother or alone. He probably had a history of mental illness and probably had been hospitalized or institutionalized for his mental condition. In addition, the profile suggested that once the offender was apprehended, the interrogators might try to establish a personal relationship with him.

Within 6 weeks, three other elderly women were attacked. All had lived within a 1-mile radius of the original attack. Of these three women, the first was 70 years old. She was stabbed 21 times in the neck with such force and rage that a half inch of the scissors was left lodged in her neck. The next victim, who was also attacked in her home, was stabbed in the neck 11 times. The last victim succeeded in warding off the attacker and called the police. A suspect was apprehended.

In the course of the interrogation, the suspect admitted that he had been in the homes of the victims. In the case of the decapitated victim, he denied stabbing her but did say that he had "killed a demon" that had been chasing him. Elaborating on his story, he stated that the only time he was safe from the demon that had been after him was when he was on a city bus or in jail. On the evening of the first attack he got off a bus, and the demon was there waiting for him. He ran and entered the house at the first door he came to. The demon ran past him and then into the victim's bedroom. The killer grabbed a butcher knife from the kitchen, ran into the bedroom, and repeatedly stabbed the demon.

The profile in this case was accurate. The amount of evidence, the chaos evident in the crime scene, the weapon's belonging to the victim as well as its being left at the crime scene, the violence done to the victim, the lack of restraints, the body left at the death scene—all suggested a profile that did indeed narrow the scope of the investigation. (first author's files)

Organized nonsocial offenders and disorganized asocial offend-ers also tend to have different relationships to their victims. Both types select "strangers" as victims, but the character of the strangers is different. The disorganized asocial offender may be aware before the crime of the existence of his victim, but he has no personal relationship with that person. In the case related above, for example, the killer lived in the neighborhood and knew the addresses and locations of the apartments in which the murders occurred. For the organized nonsocial offender, however, the victim is a targeted stranger. One offender told the first author in an interview about his typical choice for a victim:

> If I had made a composite of my "typical" victim, it would read like this: The individual would be white, female, between the ages of 13 and 19, given the adolescent dress and manner. I would say that perhaps 75% of my victims fell under this general description. Obviously there is a pattern of selectivity here, else this large percentage figure would not so closely fit the description I've laid forth. Just as obviously, it wasn't a matter of my victims' "just being there."
>
> But just how conscious was this selectivity and why did roughly three-quarters of my victims fit this mold? In answer to the first question, I would have to say that it was not entirely conscious in that I didn't hold a general picture of an 18-year-old adolescent, white female in my mind. Certainly more and more often than not, I was roaming the streets in search of females in general, but with no specific age group in mind. Yet 75% of the time the person who "clicked" and "registered" in my mind was the girl I described above. More accurately, I was reacting to the "click" in my gut, more so than to predetermined, sought-after characteristics. Yet the predisposition toward victims of that general description, subconscious or not, was there.

This violent personal offender seemed to have some understanding of the reason for his selection of young white females. He went on to discuss how he was rejected in high school by very popular female students. Of another nationality, he was averse to dating young women of his own ethnic group, and he provided some insight into this reluctance, citing some shame about his own background. The slightest resistance to his social overtures met with rage.

Minimal conversation takes place usually between the disorganized offender and his victim. It is a blitz attack, and the establishment of any relationship is not a requirement. In contrast, conversation between the organized offender and his victim is a language of intimidation once the victim is within the offender's "comfort zone."

The vehicle for the initial contact now becomes the vehicle for control. The organized nonsocial offender appears able to assay the vulnerability of his stalked victim. One serial killer remarked, "I can tell by the way they walk, the way they tilt their heads. I can tell by the look in their eyes" (first author's files).

Victims of organized nonsocial offenders often suffer vicious attacks prior to death. Sometimes these offenders use restraints to render their victims helpless and to heighten victims' fear, which the offenders may need to see in order to gain full satisfaction. Disorganized offenders, in contrast, usually have no need for restraints, because their purpose is not to intimidate or to instill fear. One organized offender described to the first author his reaction to one victim's failure to show the fear he wanted to see:

> When I sighted the women [his two victims] they meant absolutely *nothing* to me as human beings. Indicative of the worthlessness they held in my eyes was my extreme rage toward the first woman, who I felt was defying me through her "unwillingness" to "suffer well." Undoubtedly she was instead paralyzed by cold and fear, but, in my own distorted mind, her silence and lack of struggling was a defiant sign against being reduced to brokenness and worthlessness, and therefore, the contempt I felt for her defiance was such that I killed her right away, forgetting her almost instantly as I went to the second woman.

In an organized nonsocial crime scene, normally the weapon not only belongs to the offender but is taken from the crime scene. This is not true of the disorganized asocial offender. This violent personal offender does not think through what he is about to do; the act is spontaneous. Bringing a weapon to a crime scene shows at least some form of rudimentary planning, and this offender does not think ahead.

The moving of a body from the crime scene may be an indication that the unknown suspect is an organized nonsocial type. The disorganized type has no desire or need to move the body. Once the killing has been accomplished, his mission is over.

CONCLUSION

In this chapter we have discussed a typology of offenders that has important implications for law enforcement profiling of lust killers. We have addressed the typical personal characteristics and postoffense behaviors of disorganized asocial and organized nonsocial offenders, as well as the interviewing techniques recommended for use with each type of suspect. We have also discussed the differences that may be found in the crime scenes associated with the two types of offenders.

Investigators will find the guidelines laid out in the typology discussed here to be useful in their profiling of violent crimes, as they take into account the chaos or lack of chaos in a crime scene, the presence or absence of a weapon, the presence or absence of mutilation of the victim, and other details.

Of course, not all crimes are lust killings. In the next chapter we will address the use of profiling in suspected serial murder cases.

NOTES

1. The FBI also has dropped the words *nonsocial* and *asocial* from the labels in its typology, but, as explained, we retain both terms here because we believe they have important meanings.

2. See Chapter 6 for a discussion of staging, signatures, and other elements of crime scene assessment as they pertain to organized and disorganized offenders.

6. Profiling Serial Murderers

The motives, gains, and etiology of serial murder differ from those of other forms of homicide. Fundamentally different from conventional homicide, serial murder claims more than 5,000 victims a year by an estimated 35 serial murderers currently at large in the United States (Holmes & De Burger, 1988; Norris & Birnes, 1988, pp. 15, 19; A. Rule, personal communication, May 21, 1985). Some researchers assert that as many as one-third of all yearly homicides are attributable to serial killers (Linedecker & Burt, 1990, p. ix). It has been suggested that serial murder is on the rise (Gammage, 1991), and that there is an epidemic of such homicides, as reflected in a statement made by Robert Ressler, a retired FBI agent who was instrumental in the formation of the Bureau's Behavioral Science Unit: "Serial killing—I think it's at epidemic proportion. The type of crime we're seeing today did not really occur with any known frequency prior to the fifties. An individual taking ten, twelve, fifteen, twenty-five, thirty-five lives is a relatively new phenomenon in the crime picture of the U.S." (Jenkins, 1994, p. 67). Some scholars have expressed the fear that such statements may cause some members of the public to become unduly alarmed (Sears, 1991), and some believe that authors in this field are deliberately creating their own monster (Jenkins, 1994).

It would be an error to assume that we are all potential victims of serial killers, or that there is a serial killer around every corner. However, from our own experiences with police departments across the United States, we believe that current estimates concerning numbers of victims may be too high, but estimates of numbers of killers may actually be too low. In lecturing across the country, the first author seldom comes away from a lecture site without a police officer telling him about a serial murderer he had previously not known about. It is our estimate that there are at least 100 serial murderers currently active in the United States. Estimates of the numbers of victims have been questioned by many experts, including Egger (1990), Jenkins (1994, pp. 20-29, 60-64; 1995), and Hickey (1991). It should be kept in mind that some serial killers may kill no more than one victim a year, or none at all during particular periods of time (perhaps because they are prevented from doing so by illness or incarceration). But there is no doubt that a substantial number of the victims who fall prey to serial predators, including killers, each year are not recognized as serialists' victims because of lack of communication among law enforcement agencies ("linkage blindness"; Egger, 1990), law enforcement turf issues, and some law enforcement personnel's simple refusal to identify or accept some cases as instances of serial murder.

The number of victims any given murderer has is a defining characteristic for applying the label of serial killer. The most common number given is a minimum of three victims (Holmes, 1988); however, some researchers, such as Jenkins (1994), prefer to reserve the label for killers of four or more persons, and others believe the number should be as low as two. If two were to be adopted by authorities and those within the criminal justice system as the defining number, clearly the number of offenders defined as serial killers would increase drastically.

TYPOLOGY OF SERIAL MURDERERS

Despite the similar motivations of all humans, individuals behave differently from each other (Drukteinis, 1992). These differences derive from a variety of factors. As stated earlier, social and behav-

TABLE 6.1 Spatial Mobility and Serial Murderers

Geographically Stable	*Geographically Transient*
Lives in same area for some time	Travels continually
Kills in same or nearby area	Travels to confuse law enforcement
Disposes of bodies in same or nearby area	Disposes of bodies in far-flung areas

ioral scientists have formulated models to explain the behavior of various categories of people. The typology of serial murderers presented below has been developed based on interviews with and case studies of serial murderers, many of whom are currently incarcerated in U.S. prisons (Holmes & De Burger, 1985, 1988).

SPATIAL MOBILITY OF SERIAL KILLERS

The initial distinction that may be made among serial murderers is in their degree of spatial mobility (see Table 6.1). Some serial murderers live in one area and kill in that same area or a nearby area. These offenders are termed *geographically stable* killers. There are many examples of this type of killer: John Wayne Gacy (Chicago), Wayne Williams (Atlanta), Ed Gein (Plainfield, Wisconsin), and many more. *Geographically transient* serial murderers, in contrast, travel a great deal in their killings. These offenders will cruise, not necessarily to look for victims, but, more important, to avoid detection. As several serial killers have told us in personal interviews, if you are looking for victims, you can find them down the block. Geographically transient offenders log thousands of miles a year in their cars in pursuit of murder. They travel to avoid detection and to confuse law enforcement. Henry Lucas (Cox, 1991), Ted Bundy, Larry Eyler (Kolarik, 1992), and Chris Wilder (Gibney, 1990) are all examples of transient serial killers. See also the work of Hickey (1991), who adds a "place specific" trait to the typology predicated upon mobility.

THE VISIONARY SERIAL KILLER

Most serial murderers are not psychotic; they are definitely in touch with reality and respond to that reality. Such nonpsychotic killers tend to be psychopathic; that is, they possess a character disorder. By contrast, the visionary serial killer is propelled to kill by voices he hears or visions he sees. These breaks from reality demand that he kill certain kinds of people. This type of killer is "outer-directed" by these voices, sometimes from an apparition of the devil or a demon. Harvey Carignan was convinced that God spoke to him, demanding he kill young women. He judged women to be "evil," and he believed he was God's instrument in killing them (author's files).

The visions and the voices experienced by the visionary serial killer may be perceived to be from God or the devil. The visions and voices legitimate for the offender his violence against others, who are usually strangers to him. This kind of offender is truly out of touch with reality. In psychiatric terms, he is psychotic. A competent defense attorney for this kind of killer will typically encounter little difficulty in having his client declared "insane" or "incompetent" in court.

The visionary serial killer does not engage in any crime scene "staging," or the deliberate altering of the crime scene to disguise the manifest purpose in the commission of the crime (Douglas, Burgess, Burgess, & Ressler, 1992).

THE MISSION SERIAL KILLER

The mission serial killer feels a need on a conscious level to eradicate a certain group of people. This type of offender is not psychotic; he does not hear voices or see visions. He is very much in touch with reality, lives in the real world, and interacts with that world on a daily basis. However, he acts on a self-imposed duty to rid the world of a class of people: prostitutes, Catholics, Jews, young black males, or any other identifiable group. Such a killer may be either an organized nonsocial personality or a disorganized asocial type, but the former is more typical. Usually, when such an offender is arrested for his crimes, his neighbors are amazed at what he has done, often saying such things as, "He was such a fine young man."

In one recent case, four young women were murdered in similar ways. One was a known prostitute, and the others had alleged reputations for casual sexual encounters. The way they dressed appeared to convey their sexual availability and their willingness to participate in impersonal sex for money. The murderer of these women had a personal mission to rid his community of prostitutes. A suspect was arrested, and during his interrogation he showed not only an awareness of his killings, but a sense of pride based on the service he felt he had done for his community in eliminating such women.

THE HEDONISTIC SERIAL KILLER

The lust or thrill killer, a subtype of the category of hedonistic serial killer, has made a vital connection between personal violence and sexual gratification. This connection of sex with violence is firmly established, and the offender realizes sexual gratification through the homicide. These offenders murder because they derive pleasure from the act; killing is for them an eroticized experience.

Because of the pleasure he gets from killing, this type of hedonistic killer's crimes are process focused, generally taking some time to complete, in contrast with the quick kill more characteristic of a visionary or a mission murderer, whose crimes may be described as act focused. The processed-focused killing of the hedonistic murderer may include anthropophagy, dismemberment, necrophilia, torture, mutilation, domination, or other fear-instilling activities. Jerry Brudos, for example, surgically removed one foot from his first victim and dismembered the breasts of two other victims. He made epoxy molds from the breasts and mounted the molds on his fireplace mantle (Stack, 1983). Ken Bianchi and Angelo Buono took young women to Buono's home for the purpose of torture and murder. Often they covered their victims' heads with plastic bags until they passed out, reviving them later to continue their savage ritual (O'Brien, 1985). The hedonistic serial killer receives sexual pleasure from such interaction with a helpless victim. Other killers who may be classified as hedonistic include Robert Berdella (Jackman & Cole, 1992) and Jeffrey Dahmer (Baumann, 1991), as well as John Gacy (Cahill, 1986; Sullivan & Maiken, 1983).

Another type of serial killer who may also be classified as a hedonistic killer does not have sexual gratification as a prime motive. This is the *comfort-oriented* serial murderer, who kills for personal gain. Professional assassins, for instance, kill because there is profit to be realized from their behavior. Other comfort killers may kill for profit people to whom they are related or with whom they have some kind of relationship; H. W. Mudgett, for instance, killed a variety of people—wives, fiancees, employees—to collect monies and properties. Usually, women who are serial killers are of this type; Aileen Wuornos (Kennedy & Nolin, 1992) and Dorothea Puente (Blackburn, 1990) are examples.

Apprehension of lust or thrill hedonistic serial murderers can be especially difficult if they are geographically transient. Their methods of killing make investigation of these crimes troublesome. Also, often this type of killer is intelligent, and if he is geographically mobile, his apprehension may be delayed for years.

THE POWER/CONTROL SERIAL KILLER

The power/control killer receives sexual gratification from the complete domination of his victim. As one serial murderer told the first author in an interview, "What more power can one have than over life and death?" Contrary to one description of the killing of a young woman that reported the serial killer's sexual pleasure connected with the act, the integral origin of pleasure for this kind of killer is not sexual; it is the killer's ability to control and exert power over his helpless victim (Michaud & Aynesworth, 1983). He derives his gratification from the belief that he has the power to make another human being do exactly what he wants. By dominating his victims completely, he experiences a "sexual" pleasure akin to the pleasure of the hedonistic serial murderer of the lust or thrill subtype.

This murderer is psychologically rooted in reality. Like the hedonistic killer, he does not suffer from a mental disease; however, a case may be made for a diagnosis of sociopathy or character disorder. This type of killer is aware of social rules and cultural guidelines, but he chooses to ignore them. Like a true sociopath, he lives by his own personal rules and guidelines.

The killing of the power/control murderer is process focused; he will prolong the killing scene because of the psychological gain he gets from this process. Like the overwhelming number of serial killers, this type will kill with hands-on weapons; he especially has a tendency to strangle his victims.

SERIAL MURDERERS: GENERAL CHARACTERISTICS

There should be a careful distinction drawn between the characteristics of serial murderers and the causes of serial murder. It is important to distinguish among the various types of serial killers as well as to inventory the characteristics of such murderers. In this context, *characteristics* are what appear to be commonalities among certain types of killers; *causes* are elements that may explain why certain behaviors occur (Holmes & De Burger, 1985).

It is impossible to speak in absolute terms when dealing with aberrant personalities (Blair, 1993), but the following generalizations may be asserted. The majority of serial killers appear to share certain characteristics: They tend to be male, white, in the age range of 25-34, intelligent (or at least street-smart), charming and charismatic, and police groupies or interested in police work. A perfect example of the embodiment of these characteristics was Ken Bianchi, a white male and a private security officer and applicant for a police department; he was intelligent, charming, and young. Ottis Toole, however, is on the other end of the continuum. By no stretch of the imagination could he be called charming or intelligent, and he was older than the average serial killer when he committed his crimes. One serial killer on death row in the same prison as Toole told the first author that Toole has the "IQ of Cool Whip."

As a serial killer's crimes progress, there appears to be a general tendency toward personality degeneration. There is less and less planning, and although the time between the killing episodes decreases, the episodes increase in violence. Again, witness the case of Jerry Brudos. Brudos's second murder occurred 11 months after his first, and the third occurred 4 months after the second; his last killing occurred less than a month later. Brudos amputated the left foot of his first victim, the left breast of his second victim, and both breasts of the third victim; he sent electrical shocks throughout his last known victim's body.

A SERIAL MURDERER'S PERSPECTIVE

From the minds and emotions of serial killers comes the "truth" of serial murder. Unfortunately, most killers are either unwilling to talk freely about their crimes or are working on court appeals and do not feel free to talk about their cases and their emotions. This has proven to be true for most of the serial murderers who have been interviewed. However, one convicted serial killer who felt the need to talk freely about what he had done consented to speak with the first author; the following material is drawn from the taped interview that resulted. The interview took place in a small interviewing room normally reserved for attorneys to talk with their imprisoned clients. The interviewee said that he had killed scores of people, but would not elaborate on the details of those crimes because of the lack of legal confidentiality attached to such an interview. He did say, however, that he felt he was an authority on serial murder, if for no other reason than that he was one himself. The complete interview lasted 8 hours.

My comments pertain to various inner workings of serial murderers, offered from the perspective of someone who has been just such a killer: myself. There are various types of serial killers, so it is obvious that my input here will not be directly applicable to each and every murderer who bears that appellation. But there are many of this fold who, while appearing intelligent and rational and essentially normal to the unsuspecting eye, are nonetheless driven by a secret, inner compulsion to seize upon other human beings, usually complete strangers, for the purpose of subjecting them to deliberate terror, systematic brutalization, and then death. This is the type of killer I was. This is the type of killer I've endeavored to understand through many years of introspection. And it is upon the inner workings of this form of murderer—the sadistic serial killer—that I hope to present some insights for those who might benefit from my own unique, albeit unenviable, perspective.

VICTIM SELECTION

Among the issues I have heard discussed regarding serial killers is that of their victim selection process. The traditional school of thought has it that serial murderers, on the whole, select their victims on the basis of certain physical and/or personal characteristics which they, the victims, possess. This assertion presupposes that, within the mind of each individual serial killer, there evolves a synthesis of preferred characteristics and, ultimately, a clear, specific picture of his ideal victim—male or female, black or white, young or old, short or tall, large-busted or small, shy or forward, and so on. Then, as the reasoning goes, when a typical serial killer begins an active search for human prey, he will go to great lengths to capture and victimize only those individuals who closely fit the mold of his preferred "ideal."

I am personally convinced that every serial killer does indeed nurture a rather clear mental picture of his own ideal victim. However restrained the outer demeanor of many a serial murderer may appear, each is without question a hyperactive and exacting thinker, this thought-life obsessively preoccupied with the smallest details of how and what he will do to his future victims. For throughout each one, he pays particular attention to the varied modes of restraint, abuse, and destruction that will later be his options when a victim is on hand, his mind all the while deciding which of these options provide him the most in the way of self-gratification. And, just as he focuses so attentively upon the methods of violence which gratify the most, so does he pay close attention to those physical details and personal characteristics which he has determined, through his imagination, to be the ones most gratifying to find and abuse as the objects of his later violence. The ideal methods and the ideal victim, then, are fairly well established in the mind of a serial killer long before he actually seeks out his prey.

Notwithstanding this point, however, I strongly believe that in the case of most serial killers, the physical and personal characteristics of those on their respective list of victims only infrequently coincide with the desired traits of their imagined "ideal." In my own case, a host of assorted factors contributed to what I finally deemed to be my ideal victim, this mental vision consisting of such specific traits: gender, sex, race, size, shape, age, length and color of hair, dress, and certain characteristics concerning my ideal victim's bearing. Yet, despite this collection of "preferred" traits, none of my actual victims ever completely fit the mold of my "ideal," and only a very tiny fraction possessed slightly more than half of the desired characteristics. The remainder of my victims fit no discernible mold or pattern whatsoever, beyond their common trait of gender. And such is the case, I believe, with most serial killers—their ideal victim, and those whom they actually victimize, seldom are one and the same.

There are two basic, interrelated reasons for this disparity. The first centers on the extreme caution exercised by a serial killer in his predatory search for a victim; the second, upon the nature of the compulsion that drives him to violence.

Addressing the first reason, it can be said that a serial killer is among the most alert and cautious of all human beings, this arising from his foremost concern to carry out his activities at the very lowest minimum of risk to himself. However, as much as he has inwardly justified his intentions, he nevertheless *does* have an unacknowledged sense or awareness of the heinous nature of the acts he will commit. He is aware of the stakes involved—that there is absolutely no room for error—and therefore will mark out no one for capture unless he perceives the odds to be overwhelming in his favor. His motto might well be, "Whom I cannot seize safely and with ease, I will not seize at all."

This unremitting sense of caution has direct ramifications on victim selection in that, during the course of his search for human prey, a serial killer is seldom apt to find his preferred ideal victim in a position of safe and easy capture. However obsessed he may be with capturing his "ideal," he is frequently thwarted by the simple fact that, in actual practice, the opportunity for this hardly ever presents itself under the requisite circumstances demanded by his extreme caution. In truth, it is a difficult and time-consuming task to locate any potential victim who can be readily seized without risk of detection. And it is a task made all the more difficult and time-consuming when the parameters of selectivity are narrowed by any focus upon an "ideal." A serial killer could, of course, bide his time. He could reject all other easy prey until, at last, his ideal victim appeared in circumstances perfectly suited to his caution. In actual practice, however, he rarely will choose to wait very long.

Why is this so? Because as the second reason given earlier, the nature of a serial murderer's compulsion for violence is such that it precludes any prolonged or self-imposed delay in acting out his brutal urges. Initially, he may set out fully determined to succeed at capturing his ideal victim regardless of how long he might have to remain on the prowl. But, as time passes without his promptly accomplishing this specific end—a common occurrence within his many hunts—his ballooning compulsion for violence itself will swiftly overtake any initially held obsession for a particular mold of victim.

This speedy shift of a serial killer's priorities might be likened to the conduct of a lion who finds himself hungry for a meal. Stirred to the hunt by his initial pangs of hunger, the lion sets out in search of gazelle—that is, gazelle in particular—because he happens to favor the taste of gazelle meat over all other savanna fare. Early in his hunt, a hyena and then a zebra cross well within his killing range, but the lion lets them both pass unmolested and continues on with his search for the preferred gazelle. As time passes, however, he finds that the gazelles just won't cooperate; they smartly keep their distance each time the lion nears, remaining safely outside his killing range. His hunger and frustration mounting with every passing moment, the lion quickly decides that *any* meal will do, be it a skimpy long-eared hare or a sickly emaciated monkey. In the end, it's the *meal,* not the *type* of meal that really counts.

So it is with a serial murderer. A serial killer just will not defer acting out his violent urges simply because his ideal victim ada-mantly refuses to materialize at his beck and call. Instead, his intense and mounting hunger for real-life violence against a real-life captive inevitably compels him to settle for any soonest-available victim of opportunity. And it is this, the increasingly mounting stresses of a serial killer's compulsivity, and not such concerns as preferred physi-cal or personal characteristics, which ultimately determines the mat-ter of victim selectivity.

PERCEPTION OF POTENTIAL VICTIMS

As a serial killer steps away from his home to begin a hunt for human prey, it is almost always true that he knows absolutely nothing about the person who is fated to become his next victim. And, in truth, he really doesn't care. He doesn't care whether the stranger he'll soon encounter is a person of hopes and fears, likes and dislikes, past

disappointments and goals for the future. He doesn't care whether
the person loves or is loved. Indeed, he doesn't even care whether
the person has a name. All such personal characteristics fall within
the sphere of real-life human beings. And, as far as he is concerned,
his next victim is not at all a human being in the accepted sense of
the term. So, well before he ever crosses paths with his next victim,
he has already stripped that person of all human meaning and worth;
he has unilaterally decreed, in absentia, that the person is deserving
of no human consideration whatsoever.

This, then, is a serial killer's personal perception of all his future
victims; each one is nothing more than a mere object, depersonalized
in advance, with each existing only for himself and only to be seized
and used as he sees fit. Moreover, he perceives his unseen prey not
just as objects to be used, but as objects worthy of extreme contempt,
vicious abuse, and certain destruction. In the mind of a serial killer,
nothing is more worthless, and no one is more contemptuous, than
the nameless, faceless stranger for whom he sets out to hunt.

Why does a serial killer hold such an extreme and irrational
disregard for others? How can he so utterly despise and count
worthless another human being whom he has even yet to meet? The
answer to these questions is that, after years of nurturing and reinforcing his compulsion for violence within his imagination, each
serial killer comes to a place where he finds it absolutely necessary
to act out his brutal mind-images. And this, in turn, thrusts him into
the position of needing to perceive living human beings—the only
pool from which he can obtain real-life victims—as worthless objects
deserving the violence he desires to mete out. So, he mentally
transforms them into hateful creatures, because, in the twisted mo-
rality of his own making, it is only against such that he can justifiably
and joyfully inflict his manifestly hateful deeds of violence.

Naturally, this outlook does not arise spontaneously or overnight.
A serial murderer does not just wake up one fine morning with the
desire to hate and kill other human beings. Instead, the entire sum of
his initial violent activity takes place only in his imagination, and
usually minus the presence of any outwardly directed feelings of
hatred. At first, he is perhaps only intrigued by the mind-pictures he
allows into his imagination. Then, gradually these begin to provide
him with a sense of pleasure and self-gratification, this arising from
the heady sense of control and power and accomplishment he feels
as he places himself in the role of the aggressor within his make-
believe arena of violence. He perhaps cannot identify or articulate
these sensations for what they are, but, to him, all that matters is that

they *feel good,* and so he continues mentally playing out the violence that causes them to surface. For the moment, however, his "victims" remain wholly imaginary, and he is content enough with this arrangement. Thus, at this early stage, he almost certainly gives no serious thought to the possibility of carrying out violence over to actual, living victims.

As he continues dwelling on such images, however, he becomes like the budding heroin addict who finds he requires a more powerful jolt, a more powerful means of self-gratification. And it is at some point during this stage that a future serial murderer begins taking the steps that will help transform his undeveloped appetite for mental violence into a full-bloom compulsion for the same. Gradually, he grows more and more dissatisfied with the limited collection of mind-pictures that his imagination has worn out to excess, so he begins to search out newer and more sophisticated imagery to play out in his mind. This imagery—which he obtains from books, magazines, movies, or any other sources depicting new examples and new methods of violence—is introduced and tried out upon his still-imaginary victims, this further reinforcing mental violence as his primary means of self-fulfillment.

The next step in the progression is that violence upon imaginary victims, however refined this violence may be, begins to lose its gratifying effects upon the future serial killer. Thus, he switches gears anew and starts practicing his mental violence on real, living people—people he sees or knows from his school, his neighborhood, or his workplace—these taking the place of what previously had always been fictional, imaginary victims. At the start of this new trend, he is probably convinced that, despite the fact that he might actually enjoy inflicting real violence upon, say, the librarian from his school, or on the girl who lives next door, he still would never consider doing such a thing to them, or to any other living human being, outside the space of his own imagination. As much as he might believe this lie, however, this imaginary brutalization of actual human beings has fateful ramifications on the course of future events. For in order to inflict injury upon the librarian or the girl next door, even if meant to be done strictly within his mind, he first and necessarily learns techniques that will later be used to sanction actual and willful victimization. This is exactly what he does, and he continues reinforcing the development of these techniques as he plays out, in his mind-pictures, his new game of replacing imaginary victims with real people. But even this new practice soon loses its novelty and gratifying effects. And, in part because he is now equipped with some experience at depersonalizing others, his deterring inhibitions gradually begin to dissolve in the face of his need for a more effective stimulus. For the first time, he begins seriously considering the thought of real violence against live human beings.

Finally, then, the decisive moment of choice arrives, and the inevitable occurs. He has practiced violence in his mind for so long and has derived such intense feelings of personal fulfillment from this imagery that his appetite for this, when it arises, is virtually insatiable. Imagery, however, no longer cuts the mustard. The future serial killer knows now that his brutal fantasies must be acted out, that only this real violence will give him the measure of relief that his compulsion craves. And, just as he never denied himself relief in the past, so will he not deny himself relief in the present. Indeed, by this time, he finds it psychologically impossible to deny himself the relief which now can come only through literal violence.

And so he crosses over the line and begins to look upon other human beings as potential victims, and as the mere props they must later become on the stage of his acted-out violence. And as he continues thinking about them, he grows to despise them, even if for no other reason than they are walking free somewhere, as yet uncaptured, thereby denying him the relief he craves and is convinced he deserves. They are "denying" him and he "deserves" them. By these and other such twisted rationalizations, he provides for himself all the reasons he needs to justify hunting people down as if they were vermin.

All such self-serving justifications, of course, are nothing but willful self-delusion and deliberate lies. To a serial killer, however, such lies are entirely necessary. For deep inside of himself, each serial murderer does have an unacknowledged awareness of the fact that his future victims are innocent human beings deserving nothing of his wrath. Yet to admit to this fact directly, he would also have to openly admit that he—and the violence he intends to inflict—is altogether unjust and wrong. And, for a man grown accustomed to the goodness and the pleasure it provides, any such admission of actual wrong is intolerable. Not only intolerable, but impossible.

PERCEPTIONS DURING VIOLENCE

Once a serial killer is in possession of a live victim, the acts he carries out on this person are very often done as if on autopilot, these almost always being a close reenactment of what he previously did only in his imagination. The reason for this is that he already knows from the countless mental scenarios of his past the degree of self-gratification he can obtain through certain specific acts and specific methods of violence. So, from among all these violent fantasies, he picks and chooses the individual cruelties, which he feels will assure the most in the way of self-fulfillment. These selections, then, comprise the process from start to finish that he carries out upon the victim he has on hand.

Yet, if the serial killer places this kind of special emphasis on the careful and systematic acting out of his favorite mind-pictures, it is only because of the tremendous meaning and pleasure he derives from watching the degrading, dehumanizing effects they have on his victims as he methodically carries them out. To him, nothing is more important than to see his victim reduced to the very lowest depths of misery and despair. For if there is any single reason for why a serial killer does what he does, it is so he may feel enlarged and magnified in his own eyes through the willful and violent degradation of another human being.

This need for self-magnification is always, I believe, a mandatory prerequisite to any episode of violence. Just prior to his every decision to victimize, a serial killer always first experiences a sudden and precipitous psychological fall, an extreme low, which he can neither tolerate nor deal with in any rational fashion. Throughout his day-to-day existence, all of his meaning is derived from the fact that he thinks himself profoundly special, unique, and perfect over all other human beings on the face of the earth. So, with the sudden onset of this mental low, he finds it virtually impossible to respond to it, especially to the crushing sense of anomie it gives rise to with anything else but unbridled inner rage. And it is this very same boiling rage that, in turn, fires up and triggers his preestablished compulsion for violence. The acting out of his cherished fantasies, he knows, will elevate him from his intolerable and infuriating psychological low; they will make things "all right" and cause him to feel good about himself; they will "prove," without any shadow of doubt, that he is really *somebody.*

This, then, aids in understanding the motivations and perceptions of a serial killer as he performs his actual deeds of violence. For when he finally has a live and helpless victim on hand, the violence he inflicts is not carried out just for the sake of violence alone, but, more so, for the purpose of reestablishing and reaffirming his own great worth via the brutal degradation of his victim. The long experience of his imaginary violence has already reinforced and "proved" the notion that, to become a *real somebody,* he needs only to display his power to debase, his power to break, and his power to destroy whomever he succeeds at capturing. So, in the twisted logic of a serial killer, he "proves" his own personal power and superiority by "proving" his victim's "worthlessness" through the demeaning violence he metes out.

The specific methods of violence he chooses to act out, then, are perceived as "good" and "righteous," perfectly appropriate for the present, as they have already been tried and tested in the imagination for their ability to restore his feelings of supremacy. And, once he actually begins, he is so intensely focused upon the careful perform-ance of this scriptlike process, and upon the restorative sensations they give rise to, that he leaves virtually no room whatsoever for perceiving his victim as anything other than a mere object, a lowly stage prop, a piece of meat necessary only for the literal acting out of his own self-serving drama.

The consequences of this outlook are that the struggles, the pain, and the outcries of a serial killer's victim inspire nothing in the way of pity; his victim is a worthless object, wholly depersonalized, and is therefore ineligible for such a human expression as pity. Rather than empathy, a serial killer feels a tremendous surge of excitement and euphoria at the sight of his victim's anguish, for this, to him, is what the whole violent episode is all about. His victim's misery is the elixir that thrills him beyond all measure, for it is his tangible assurance that all is proceeding according to his well-ordered plan; it is his visible "evidence" that he is the magnificent, all-powerful creature he always knew himself to be.

His real gratification comes from the subjugation, terrorization, and brutalization of his victim, and almost not at all from the actual murder of the victim. Thus, from a serial killer's viewpoint, his victim might be likened to a disposable paper cup, from which he takes a long and satisfying drink of water. Once the water is gone, his thirst quenched, the cup has served its purpose; it is useless and therefore can be crushed without thought and thrown away, as if it never existed. Similarly, once a serial killer's violence has run its course, providing the desired self-fulfillment, his battered victim is of no more use to him than a soggy, used-up paper cup. Since he no longer needs to terrorize or abuse, his victim is perceived as an object of inconvenience, a worn-out piece of luggage he no longer needs.

ANALYSIS OF THE PSYCHE OF A SERIAL KILLER

Although it would be a mistake to say that all serial killers think alike, it would also be foolhardy to assume that there are not some

Distorted Thinking

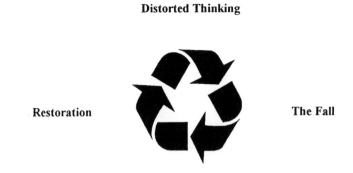

Restoration · The Fall

Negative Outward Response   Negative Inward Response

Figure 6.1. Model of Personal Violence

similarities among them. These similarities have important implications for psychological profiling. The initiation of the "process" of violence must depend on some external force or forces. The external stimuli may be either real or imagined, and the reality of the stimuli is important only to the violent offender.

As depicted in Figure 6.1, the usual psychological stage of the serial killer is *distorted thinking* (Stage 1). In this position, the killer is in a positive psychological equilibrium state. He is not in a position to ponder the repercussions of deviance because he has either blotted out the consequences or is at this time more interested in the intrinsic or extrinsic rewards of his behavior.

The serial killer will show many faces to society. Given that many (excluding visionary killers) are sociopaths, they use their charm to disarm others and to keep themselves in distorted thinking. No one, however, even the most charming, can remain in distorted thinking forever. Sooner or later, reality is going to challenge his position, and he will tumble into *the fall* (Stage 2). It may be one thing or an accumulation of events, real or imaginary, that set in motion the serial killer's movement into this second stage. For example, if A, B, C, D, and E are incidents, and event E sets the killer into the motion of the fall, then A, B, C, and D helped to set the stage for the fall. Event E might be trivial, but for the violent offender it becomes all important. The stimulus may be personal or impersonal, but *the reaction is always personal.* The killer will store these incidents deep within his psyche because his ego is so large. The violent reaction that must follow is disproportional to the event.

This is not to say that each time the serial killer reaches this stage he will respond with personal violence. Sometimes his response may be symbolic, for example, violent pornography accompanied by masturbation, but such a symbolic response can be only temporary and short-term. At some time the violent person finds physical release a necessity, and the stalking process begins. There can be no return to distorted thinking once the fall occurs.

Stage 3 is the *negative inward response.* The serial killer must deal with feelings of inadequacy, and he does so initially by mentally confronting these negative reality messages. His mental statement would be something like, "I'm too important, and I don't have to take this!" He must validate his self-status, and he will do this by the means he knows best, through the perpetration of violence. There is now the mental preparation to move to Stage 4, *negative outward response.* This becomes a compulsive and necessary element in the serial killer's self-affirmation of person superiority. At this time, the killer has no thought relating to possible consequences of his actions. Once he commences to validate and affirm his personal superiority, he is not in command. He chooses only vulnerable victims because he cannot risk a further negative reality message.

With his status once again reestablished, *restoration,* Stage 5, has been reached. Once he has entered this psychological state, the serial killer will think of the potential dangerous consequences of his behavior, and realize that he must take care in the proper disposal of the victim. Such concerns, about victim disposal, recognition, and so on, are not vital to him until he reaches Stage 5. He must now take steps to minimize his personal risk. Once he has done what he needs to do, he returns to Stage 1, distorted thinking, and the cycle is complete.

PROFILING A SERIAL MURDER CASE

No act of violence can be executed without a fantasy (Douglas et al., 1992; Sears, 1991, p. 68). The content and character of the fantasy will change from one person to another and from one type of serial killer to another. The fantasy of the visionary serial killer may center on a voice from God or a vision from hell. The sexual fantasy of the lust or thrill hedonistic serial killer may focus on a victim who is faceless.

The role and existence of the fantasy can lend some direction to the profiling process. An alert law enforcement professional investigating a case of serial murder, for example, can make use of the knowledge that a serial killer is unlikely to commit violence while in the distorted thinking phase of the cycle described above. If the murders "stop" in a case of suspected serial murder, the inference may be drawn that something positive is happening in the life of the unknown killer. Maybe he has married, and a check on recently issued marriage licenses can turn up a possible lead. Whatever the exact events, something good may have occurred within the killer's life that has enabled him to remain—if only temporarily—in the distorted thinking phase. Only when something from reality challenges him and his self-perception will he tumble into the fall and start to kill again.

ELEMENTAL TRAITS IN CRIME SCENE EVALUATION

The crime scene characteristics common to organized nonsocial offenders and disorganized asocial offenders (Douglas et al., 1992), described in Chapter 5, can be combined with the typology of serial murderers. Take, for example, the visionary serial killer. This murderer modally reflects the disorganized asocial personality. The characteristics of this killer are reflected in the crime scene itself. There is ample physical evidence, overkill, the weapon belonged to the victim and is left at the scene, and so on. The personality characteristics are also similar. He is a loner, probably lives and/or works near the crime scene, and the victim is a victim of opportunity.

The mission serial killer is more likely to be of the organized nonsocial type. This serial killer selects one type of victim, stalks his victims, probably has an anal personality, and uses his own weapon, which will usually not be found at the controlled crime scene.

Table 6.2 lists the elements of crime scenes and their relations to the various types of serial killers. Combining the typology of serial murderers laid out above with the FBI's typology of violent offenders, especially when sexual gratification is one of the prime motives in a murder, allows the profiler to make the best use of both theoretical models.

For example, the manifest motive of the power/control serial killer is the ultimate possession of his victim. Sexual gratification can take many different forms, and this serial killer's satisfaction emanates from his complete domination of his victims. Ted Bundy is an excellent example of such a killer. For the power/control serial murderer, as for other types, there are five "windows" in the killing process (see Figure 6.2). For the killing to commence, a fantasy must set the process in motion. It is not the kill that terminates the process, but the disposal of the body.

The crime scene traits listed in Table 6.2 can be examined and matched with the different types of serial killers. For example, usually a visionary, mission, or comfort serial killer will not move the body from the kill site. From a profiling point of view, the movement of the body denotes planning beforehand and after the kill itself. The physical evidence present in the kill site can be examined by the investigator. This is not to say that there is no evidence to be found in the dump site, but the movement of the body from the kill site to the dump site is in itself a valuable piece of information about the personality of the offender.

Only the visionary serial killer is not concerned with a specific victim type, because he is outwardly motivated by his voices or visions. The hedonistic, power/control, or mission serial murderer carefully selects a victim who will fulfill a psychological need or whose death will result in material gain. Only the comfort serial killer, a subtype of the hedonistic type, will kill victims with whom he or she has a

TABLE 6.2 Crime Scene Analysis of Suspected Serial Murder Cases

Crime Scene Characteristics	Type of Serial Killer					
	Visionary	Mission	Comfort	Lust	Thrill	Power/ Control
Controlled crime scene	no	yes	yes	yes	yes	yes
Overkill	yes	no	no	yes	no	no
Chaotic crime scene	yes	no	no	no	no	no
Evidence of torture	no	no	no	yes	yes	yes
Body moved	no	no	no	yes	yes	yes
Specific victim	no	yes	yes	yes	yes	yes
Weapon at the scene	yes	no	yes	no	no	no
Relational victim	no	no	yes	no	no	no
Victim known	yes	no	yes	no	no	no
Aberrant sex	no	no	no	yes	yes	yes
Weapon of torture	no	no	no	yes	yes	yes
Strangles the victim	no	no	no	yes	yes	yes
Penile penetration	?	yes	usually not	yes	yes	yes
Object penetration	yes	no	no	yes	yes	no
Necrophilia	yes	no	no	yes	no	yes
Gender usually	male	male	female	male	male	male

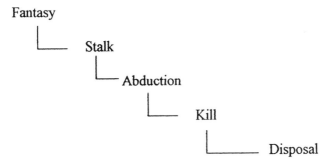

Figure 6.2. Windows in Serial Murder

relationship of some kind; the others will murder strangers, usually with hands-on weapons in a violent fashion. Pills and poison are weapons that are usually associated with the comfort killer.

The kill scene is often obviously different from the disposal site. Visionary, mission, and comfort killers will usually not move the body from where the kill itself has occurred. Therefore, if the kill site is also the disposal site, then the perpetrator is probably one who lives close to the victim and shares many of the characteristics of the disorganized asocial personality type. Table 6.2 lists selected characteristics that can be ascertained by an attentive examination of the murder scene or the disposal site.

The weapon chosen, the owner of the weapon, evidence of necrophilia, evidence of penile and/or object penetration, and other elements revealed by the crime scene can help the investigator narrow the scope of the investigation. If, for example, a series of prostitutes has been murdered and necrophilia is involved, it may very well be that the killer believes he is receiving messages from God to rid the world of such "undesirables." This becomes more of a possibility if the crime scenes reflect a great deal of chaos with accompanying physical evidence. If necrophilia is not involved, the killer's motives may be more likely to have an inner source, a characteristic of the mission serial murderer.

The profiler can gain some basic information concerning the type of offender by matching the crime and disposal scene evidence with the type of serial murder category. Although computers may be of great help with such matching and their use may soon be quite widespread, the value of the profiler's personal involvement should never be underestimated.

ADDITIONAL PROFILING ELEMENTS

The information in this section concerning crime scenes and disposal scenes has been obtained through interviews with serial murderers. It is interesting to note that the murderers have told us some things that are incongruent with the theories of profilers and those who are psychodynamically oriented, but the murderers themselves are well versed in their own killing and what they did to their victims. This information was obtained from killers whose victims numbered from fewer than 10 to "scores and scores."

BLINDFOLDS

One element in many killings is the presence of a blindfold. Blindfolds can take many forms; masks, rags, or other pieces of cloth may be used, or victims can simply be kept in total darkness. One obvious reason for a blindfold is to hide from the victim the identity of the killer. One killer said that he blindfolded his victims, none of whom he knew on a personal level or believed would recognize him, to confuse and terrorize them. There may be another dimension to the blindfolding process—it may be that it further depersonalizes and objectifies the victim. Hence, the fantasy of the serial killer is aided by the blindfold, which helps to block out the personal nature of the crime. One serial killer who was also a serial rapist described this phenomenon:

> After stripping off her clothes and tying her down to a cot, I prepared for the first part of my fantasy. [He wanted the woman to perform oral sex on him.] When I got on top of her, I felt very uncomfortable, nervous and unsettled by the woman's wide-eyed facial expression. I couldn't understand why I felt that way, but I did know I couldn't begin to go on until I covered her eyes. (first author's files)

Only after he had blindfolded her did he feel comfortable enough to proceed with his attack.

So, contrary to some common assumptions, a blindfold found at the crime scene does not necessarily mean that there was a previous personal relationship between the killer and his victim. As one murderer said in an interview, "I blindfolded my victims because faces scream at you."

ATTACKS AT THE FACE

Slapping at the face of a victim depersonalizes the attack itself. Remember the remarks Will Graham made to the Red Dragon killer: "Is there something you're ashamed of?" (Harris, 1981, p. 26). Regardless of how ruthless a violent offender may be, he is still a human being, subject to the entire range of human emotions, shame included. When he is trolling for a victim, he more or less recognizes that his pseudocontempt for this eventual captive is but a shoddy excuse to justify the hunt. And when he finally does seize a stranger to victimize, his unacknowledged awareness of his victim's actual innocence gives rise to a creeping sense of shame—or some similar emotion—which he has to deal with in order to proceed with what he *knows* is wrong.

Of course, being an expert at glossing over this emotion, he will not let this deter him from his ultimate, selfish aim. One of his key means of eliminating the "shame factor" (such as when in possession of a complete stranger), however, is to blot out the eyes, mask the identity—to keep the person a *nonperson*. When there is no "real person" to face, only a prop with a rag over its eyes, there is no shame.

On a more pragmatic level, violence directed at the face of the victim is a device manifestly intended to control. An attack at the eyes is especially important because of the obvious reason that injury can result in blindness and therefore reduce the possibility of a personal identification. This is usually not a factor in a serial murder case because the killer has already made the decision that the victim will not survive a process-oriented murder event.

Oral sex can be viewed as a further attack upon the victim's face, and a departure from the point of view that any such attack is an impersonal one. Of course, there is a utilitarian factor involved in oral sex; the offender wants his victim to arouse him sexually. In this stance, oral sex is not to be perceived as an attack; rather, as one serialist stated, oral sex "was an acceptable usage of a nameless receptacle" (first author's files).

There is an inclination to believe that oral sex by itself can reveal little in terms of whether a crime has been perpetrated by a stranger or an acquaintance of the victim. Oral sex accompanied by blindfolding, however, would seem to point to a stranger-perpetrated offense. Oral sex with no evidence of blindfolding, especially when there has also been physical battering of the victim's face, tends to point to an acquaintance-perpetrated crime.

An attack in darkness combined with a blindfold is intended to terrorize as well as to depersonalize the victim. The blindfold, while reducing some of the personal element in the violence, renders the victim a nonentity and an object, but the attack at the face brings to the fantasy level of the perpetrator a personal but stranger dimension.

DISPOSAL OF THE BODY

Lust, thrill, and power/control serial killers are the most likely kinds of serialists to dispose of the bodies of their victims. These types of killers share many of the personality attributes of the organized nonsocial personality type. The reasons they dispose of the bodies are varied, and whether the killer intends for a body to be found or not can be a factor. One serial killer, when questioned about why many victims had never been found, said, "You only find the bodies of the ones [the killer] wants you to find" (first author's files). He may have also been saying that the disposal of the body was a form of "advertisement" in his killing career.

Of those interviewed, not one serial killer related any concern about the bodies being found so that the victims' families could be relieved of doubt about their loved ones. The serial murderer is not concerned about his victims' families.

The disposal of the body is a signal that the killing process involving that particular victim is over. This completes the *windows* of serial murder, or the phases that serial killers go through in their killings. It is not a signal that the killing will start again. The murderer is now in a psychological state of euphoria, back in the distorted thinking stage of the cycle. He will remain in distorted thinking as long as reality does not challenge his position of self-importance.

For most serial murderers, learning how to dispose of bodies takes the same form as any other social learning process. In the same way one learns to do many everyday things, legal or not, the serial murderer learns the most personally beneficial manner of disposing of his victims. He will take care in the disposal because this is when he is most vulnerable. One serial murderer dumped many of his victims' bodies on a U-shaped curve in the road so that he could see both ways at the moment of his highest vulnerability.

A recent case provides an example of how a profiler's knowledge can be useful even for locating a missing body. The police in the case requested a profile from the first author, after having first called in a psychic and an astrologer, both of whom believed that the killer had taken the body through town and dumped it in a large lake on the other side of the county. The first author, in contrast, offered the opinion that the body would be found somewhere between the murder site, where the victim's purse was found, and a road where the suspected murderer was seen later the same day the victim was killed. A triangle was drawn on a map delineating the search area, and the victim's body was eventually found within that triangle by hunters looking for game. The first author's reasoning was that a killer would not risk driving through a small town where everyone knew him to dump a body in an open area near a lake—nothing mysterious, nothing magical, just a hunch based in logic, accompanied by the luck of the two hunters' find.

WEAPONS

The weapon, as well as the torture used by the killer, moves the ritualist and the victim further apart from each other as human beings. Serial killers select their weapons of murder very carefully, and usually kill with hands-on weapons for three reasons: (a) to touch the victim, (b) because the touch terrorizes the victim, and (c) because the touch degrades the victim. Hands-on weapons include straps (e.g., Jerry Brudos), women's hose (e.g., Ted Bundy), hands (e.g., Edmund Kemper), knives (e.g., Douglas Clark and Carol Bundy), hammers (e.g., Harvey Carignan), handguns (e.g., Beoria Simmons), and all other weapons that require or can be used in close contact. Fire is normally not a method preferred by serial murderers, because serial killers are socialized into the use of other weapons to kill and terrorize. This is not to say that some serial murderers will not burn their victims with cigarettes, hot spatulas, or other objects, but the final means of murder requires physical contact.

When the abduction initially transpires, the killer and the victim are close together on a social yardstick. The killer needs to establish a distance between them immediately to prove his superiority. The dispatching of a helpless and vulnerable victim is the psychological agent needed to place him back into distorted thinking.

DISMEMBERMENT

Picquerism is the repeated stabbing and wounding of a person that results in sexual gratification. Accurately, dismemberment may be viewed as a form of picquerism, so the sexual dimension of that activity cannot be ignored. Dismemberment also demonstrates and validates the power and control the killer has over his helpless victim. He is "proving" that his victim is not only nothing, but, by the complete violation of the corpse, "the victim is now little pieces of nothing," as one serial murderer stated (first author's files). This unbridled violation of the body, now a corpse, generates some form of gratification for the serial killer, either sexual satisfaction or a psychological enhancement of the ego of the murderer.

Dismemberment, as might be expected, is most typical of the lust, thrill, and power/control types of serial killer. When visionary serial killers dismember, the sexual component is generally absent; such attacks are more likely to be the result of frenzied compliance with the demands of the killer's perceived demons. Knowledge of the dichotomy of organized nonsocial offenders and disorganized asocial offenders is useful to profilers who are confronted with dismemberment as an element of a crime.

BONDAGE

The more organized the kill, the more need for bondage. The blitz attack perpetrated by visionary and mission serial killers eliminates the need for bondage, which is used primarily to render the victim helpless and in the control of the serial killer. There are at least three additional motivations for bondage: (a) to hold the victim for torture, (b) to place the victim in a degrading situation, and (c) to hurt or injure the victim. The act of being bound is itself also a form of injury.

Lust, thrill, and power/control serial killers, who connect sexual gratification with personal violence, have a need to see the distress of their struggling victims, and bondage serves this purpose.

POSITION OF THE BODY

There is also a case to be made that the positioning of the victim's body can provide important information about the serial murderer, but some care must be taken in interpreting the meaning of any positioning. The symbolic positioning of the body (e.g., in a degrading posture) may be a characteristic associated with the mission serial killer, or with the lust or thrill killer. The FBI notes that "if the [disorganized asocial] offender has mutilated the body, it may be positioned in a special way that has significance to the offender" ("Classifying Sexual Homicide," 1985).

DUCT TAPE

Since the first edition of this book was published, we have made an interesting discovery regarding an apparent relationship between the use of duct tape and the background of an offender. We have talked with several offenders in prison who have used duct tape to bind their victims; they have learned about the efficiency of duct tape for this purpose during time spent inside prison walls. They stated that other offenders instructed them not only in the manner in which the tape should be applied but also the reason for using duct tape rather than another kind of tape or heavy twine. (This method is illustrated in the movie *A Few Good Men,* when a young Marine is forcibly removed from his barracks and bound with camouflage-printed duct tape.) When duct tape is used on a murder victim, it may be an indication that the perpetrator has been in prison at some time or is a past or present member of a special services branch of the military.

STAGING

As Douglas et al. (1992) define it, "Staging is when someone purposively alters the crime scene prior to the arrival of police" (p. 251). The deliberate staging of a crime scene may be indicative of someone who is an organized killer, because it obviously takes some mental ability to realize that there is a need to change the crime scene to divert the investigation of the police. The organized offender may realize that the police will be looking for certain non-physical evidence that could indicate a certain type of offender with certain social core variables. The disorganized offender may not have the mental ability to alter a crime scene deliberately. In addition, the disorganized offender may truly not understand the investigatory process or the manner in which evidence is gathered and examined. If staging is evident in the crime scene, investigators would be wise to look for someone who fits the pattern of the organized offender rather than the disorganized one.

SOUVENIRS

The immediate reason for a serial killer to take a souvenir from a crime scene is so that he has a reminder of what has transpired. The rational decision to take a souvenir involves the same mental process as might be used by someone collecting souvenirs while on a vacation. It reminds the killer not only of the event, but of what has taken place during that event. The souvenir is also part of the psychological gain realized by the murderer during the kill. What is taken once belonged to the victim, and because of that, it is reminds the serial killer of a personal aspect of the event.

Not all serial killers take souvenirs, and those who do may not take souvenirs after every murder. The killer must make a decision to take a souvenir on a rational basis; in some cases, he may realize that there is little or no opportunity to take a part of the property of the victim without exposing himself to undue risk.

Sometimes when a serial killer takes property belonging to the victim it has less to do with the collection of souvenirs than with the prevention of identification of the victim—a way to hinder the investigation by law enforcement. If the body has been mutilated or somehow altered so that it is difficult to identify the victim, and there are no personal belongings of the victim at the scene, then the serial killer has indeed accomplished one of his purposes. The souvenir, on two levels, strips the victim of his or her identity.

TROPHIES

In the profiles the first author has submitted to police departments, he has always made a distinction between souvenirs and trophies. Trophies represent something a person has won, as a bowling trophy or a tennis trophy does. In the case of a serial murder, a trophy is something intrinsic in value; it not only represents something that has been done by the predator but also something that has value of itself. Thus, a trophy is something personal, such as a body part (e.g., a leg, a breast). A souvenir may be only a memento that recalls an experiential high point, whereas a trophy is not only a reminder of the experiential high, but a visual reward that serves as an aphrodisiac.

CONCLUSION

The initial step in creating a profile in a serial murder case is the determination that the case under investigation is truly one of serial homicide. This may sound very rudimentary, but as any investigator realizes, sometimes we all have tunnel vision, seeing only what we want to see. Once a homicide is "certified" as part of a serial murder case, the investigators must be prepared for the publicity and other ramifications that come with such a situation.

The methods, gains, and motives of serial murder are unique to each type of killer. If investigators are able to attain some understanding of the psychology of the serial killer and his propensity for violence, if they realize that the serial murderer feels that he is all-powerful and all-knowing, and that it is his birthright to feel this way, they may have a better understanding of the psychopathic serial killer. Knowledge about the nature of differing crime scenes can deepen this understanding. A chaotic or sadistic crime scene, or one in which overkill is apparent, can give investigators valuable information.

In this chapter we have attempted to fulfill two purposes for law enforcement investigators. First, we have introduced a unique typology of serial offenders that offers motives for action and evaluation of the serial killer's mind, and a particular model for personal violence. Second, we have outlined some crime scene characteristics that investigators should consider. We will address these characteristics again later in this volume.

In closing, we want to emphasize again that a profile is no substitute for a comprehensive investigation; it is simply one more investigatory aid. A profile is rarely as accurate as depicted in fictional works such as *The Red Dragon,* which is based loosely on the work of investigators John Douglas, Robert Ressler, and Ray Hazelwood. Some authors have been very negative about the value of profiling. In a scathing criticism of the FBI's Behavioral Science Unit's operation, Jenkins (1994) charges that the profiles the FBI has offered in serial murder cases have been largely unproductive. One of the Bureau's own, Paul Lindsey, has been quoted as saying, "I mean, how many serial killer cases has the FBI solved—if any?" Jenkins (1994, p. 56) even remarks that Ressler's claim that he coined the term *serial murder* is in error; Jenkins cites an earlier occurrence in the work of Lunde (1976). In the ongoing debate, it is our position that profiling should be accepted as the aid to investigation it can be.

7. Arson and Psychological Profiling

The deliberate setting of fires has a long history, as varied as the fires themselves.[1] There is no reason to believe that the motivations of all fire setters are the same or even similar (Forehand, Wierson, Frame, Kempton, & Armistead, 1991; Holt, 1994; Orr, 1989; Sakeheim & Osborn, 1986; Webb, Sakeheim, Towns-Miranda, & Wagner, 1990); arsonists are as varied as their motivations and anticipated gains. Arsonists are also different from other kinds of offenders, including property offenders and sex offenders (Kolko & Kazdin, 1992; Sakeheim, Vigdor, Gordon, & Helprin, 1985). Arsonists' motivations and planned gains can vary widely, from the purposeful offender who sets fires for monetary gain to the pyromaniac, who sets fires for erotic gratification (Law, 1991), although some researchers have pointed out that the exact role of sex as a motivating factor for arson may have been grossly exaggerated (Quinsey, Chaplin, & Upfold, 1990; Rice & Harris, 1991).

In this chapter we address the role of sexual gratification as a basic motive for the crime of arson as well as the examination of arson crime scenes for the insights they may offer into the social and demographic characteristics of arsonists.

WHAT IS ARSON?

The simple definition of arson is that it is the willful and malicious burning of property (Douglas, Burgess, Burgess, & Ressler, 1992, p. 165), but there is more to the act of arson than is revealed by this definition. The three components laid out in this definition may be elaborated as follows:

1. *Burning of property:* For the crime of arson to have occurred, the burning must be shown to be actual destruction of the target, at least in part, not just scorching (although some states include in their legal definitions of arson any physical or visible impairment of any surface).
2. *Intent:* For this element to be fulfilled, proof of the use at the fire scene of any effective incendiary device, no matter how simple, is adequate. Proof is accomplished by the ruling out of alternative possible causes.
3. *Malice:* For arson to have occurred, the intent with which the fire was started must have been malicious. That is, the arsonist had the specific intent of destroying property (DeHaan, 1991, p. 324).

Arson may be committed for a number of reasons. In an early study, Macy (1979, p. i) identified the following five types of arson:

1. Organized crime (concealing such crimes as loan sharking or extortion)
2. Insurance/housing fraud (overinsurance, block-busting, parcel clearance, gentrification, stop loss, and tax shelters)
3. Commercial (inventory depletion, modernization, and stop loss)
4. Residential (relocation, redecoration, public housing, and automobile)
5. Psychological (children and juveniles, pyromania, political, and wildlands)

One useful way to try to understand the phenomenon of arson is to examine the various types of arson and the personalities and behaviors of some types of fire setters (which we discuss later in this chapter).

Gilbert (1986, p. 444) identifies five different types of fires. First is the *natural fire,* which results from a work of nature, such as lightning. There is no form of prevention against natural fires. The second type is the *accidental fire,* which can result from faulty equipment within a structure, a person's smoking in bed, or the like. A third type is the *unknown fire,* the label applied when investigation fails to yield an exact cause. Gilbert's final two types are the *suspicious fire* and the *incendiary fire,* both of which are classified as crimes of arson.

We offer below some general statistics on arson as well as some information about the personalities and other characteristics of different kinds of arsonists and elements of which profilers should be aware in arson crime scene investigation.

STATISTICS ON ARSON

Data concerning arson are collected nationally by two federal agencies: the National Fire Protection Association (NFPA) and the Federal Bureau of Investigation. The former agency collects data concerning structural fires as well as any "suspicious" fires. The FBI's statistics are gathered from reports in which arson has been identified by the local reporting agencies. As Douglas et al. (1992) report, "The statistics compiled by both the NFPA and the FBI closely agree" (p. 164).

The U.S. Department of Justice's Bureau of Justice Statistics (1993, p. 418) reports that there were almost 20,000 crimes of arson reported in the United States in 1992. It is interesting to note that the arrest rate per 100,000 population for arson is lower than for any other Part I or Part II offense, 7.6. Table 7.1 displays further statistical data regarding arson and arsonists.

One problem with the accumulation of data is that their reliability depends upon the method by which they were collected. One might expect that all of the numbers gathered would match from agency to agency, but this does not always appear to be true. Table 7.2 presents the arson data compiled by the U.S. Department of the Treasury's Bureau of Alcohol, Tobacco and Firearms (1992) from reporting agencies.

TABLE 7.1 Arson in the United States: Arrests in 1992

Age	Total	Under 15	Under 18	18 or Older
Number	16,322	5,210	7,968	8,354
Percentage		32	49	51

Sex	Total	Male		Female
Number	16,322	14,139		2,183
Percentage		87		13

Race	Total	White	Black	American Indian or Native Alaskan	Asian or Pacific Islander
Number	16,275[a]	12,430	3,572	135	138
Percentage		76	22	.8	.8[b]

SOURCE: U.S. Department of Justice, Bureau of Justice Statistics (1993, pp. 428-432).
a. Because of unreported data, this number does not agree with previous reported total arrests.
b. Because of rounding, these figures do not total 100%.

TABLE 7.2 Arson Statistics

	1988	1989	1990	1991	1992	5 Year Total
Number of incidents	538	489	571	724	567	2,889
Number killed	55	49	143	124	52	423
Number injured	194	167	218	426	254	1,259
Property damage (in millions of dollars)	499.9	437.8	317.5	544.7	257.2	2,057.1
Insurance dollars saved (in millions)	27.8	29.7	29.4	31.7	41.3	159.9
Cases submitted	169	165	181	220	288	1,023
Defendants recommended for prosecution	389	347	354	423	478	1,991
Convicted or pled guilty	19	57	41	67	53	237

SOURCE: U.S. Department of the Treasury (1992, p. 66).

Regardless of the relative agreement of gathered data, it is apparent that arson is a very serious personal and financial problem that costs our society millions of dollars, not to mention the immeasurable cost in human lives lost because of fire setters. In the period from 1988 to 1992, more than 400 people were killed by arson fires, some intentionally, some accidentally. It is our intention here to look not only at the fires set by arsonists, but at arsonists themselves. As we develop psychological profiles of the various types of persons who intentionally set fires, it will be clear that their motivations vary, as do their social core variables and their anticipated gains.

CHARACTERISTICS OF THE FIRE SETTER

Arson is a crime that is committed almost equally often by adults and by juveniles. Some 49% of all reported cases of arson are committed by juveniles, and of these, 26% are committed by children between the ages of 10 to 14. Some 17% of adult arsonists are in the 25-34 age cohort. After the age of 35, there is a slow and gradual decrease in commission of crimes of arson.

Arson is for the most part a male crime; more than 9 of 10 arson fires are set by males. Regarding race, it seems that blacks are slightly overrepresented in comparison with their proportion in the general population; blacks account for more than one in five reported one-time arsonists but less than 10% of serial arsonists. Whites account for slightly more than three out of four arson fires, and Native Americans, Native Alaskans, Asians, Hispanics, and Pacific Islanders account for the remainder.

Sharn and Glamser (1994) reported recently in *USA Today* that of arsonists arrested, 87% had prior felony arrests, 63% had multiple felony arrests, and 24% had prior arrests for arson. Most of the arsonists lived near the scenes of their crimes: 21% lived within 5 blocks of the site, 30% lived from a half mile to a mile from the scene, 20% lived within 1-2 miles, and 16% lived more than 2 miles from where they set fires. In addition, 7% lived in institutional settings. More than 60% of the arsonists said that they had walked to their arson scenes. The motives for the arson included revenge (41%), excitement (30%), vandalism (7%), profit (5%), and concealment of a crime (5%); mixed motives accounted for 12% of the cases. These statistics should be considered by anyone beginning the process of profiling an arsonist. By combining what is typically known about arson, the various typologies of arsonists, and the principles of profiling, a profiler may develop a psychological assessment of the arsonist.

There are some basic characteristics that appear to be common to many serial arsonists. Sapp, Huff, Gary, Icove, and Horbert (n.d.) have reported statistics concerning many of these characteristics; this information is listed in Table 7.3.

TYPOLOGIES OF FIRE SETTERS

Several researchers have tried to categorize different kinds of arsonists. Rider (1980a), in reviewing the work of Lewis and Yarnell (1951), has suggested the following typology. First is the *jealousy-motivated adult male,* who sets fires in reaction to incidents that impair his vanity and impugn his personality. The next is the *would-be hero.* This fire setter rushes to the scene of a fire he himself has set so that he can appear to save lives, protect property, and so on—so he can be the apparent hero because of his swift and decisive action. These arsonists are sometimes firefighters, police officers, or others who respond to fire department calls; they may also be apparent passersby who just "happen" upon the scene. Another type of would-be hero is the volunteer fireman, who joins the department to fight fires, many of which he will set himself. The fire buff is similar to the police groupie; he wants to associate with professional firefighters, frequents the fire station, and many times is an active person in the community who has a special interest in the work of the fire department. The *excitement fire setter* ignites fires because of a need for personal excitement, but this does not include a sexual component or a sexual fantasy. The *pyromaniac,* the final type, is best understood to have a compulsive element within his personality that impels him to set fires. Other factors important to the pyromaniac's fire setting are tension reduction, pleasure, and gratification, or personality relief. Rider (1980b) reports:

The pyromaniac differs characteristically from other arsonists in that he lacks conscious motivation for his firesetting. In fact, he is

TABLE 7.3 Attributes of Serial Arsonists (in percentages)

Regular Occupation		8	5.3
menial laborer	28.2	9	13.3
retail sales worker	2.6	11	16.0
service worker	5.1	12	26.7
maintenance worker	7.7	13	1.3
police-security worker	7.7	14	4.0
fire service worker	2.6	15	1.3
office-clerical worker	10.3	16	2.7
food service worker	5.1		
homemaker	2.6	*Institutional History:*	*Mean Times*
medical service worker	5.1	*Type of Institution*	*in Institution*
		orphanage	1.3
Marital Status		foster home	1.6
single	65.9	juvenile detention	4.1
significant other	8.5	state juvenile home	1.7
married	6.1	county jail	4.9
separated	3.7	state prison	2.0
divorced	14.6	federal prison	1.3
widowed	1.2	mental health institution	3.2
		other institution	1.3
Gender			
male	94.0	*Sexual Orientation*	
female	6.0	heterosexual	75.4
		homosexual	8.7
Childhood Family Status		bisexual	15.9
both parents	57.5		
father only	3.8	*Psychological History*	
mother only	12.5	depression	3.8
father, stepmother	1.3	dyslexia	3.8
mother, stepfather	10.3	stress related	3.8
foster home	8.8	multiple diagnosis	34.6
other relatives	6.3	alcoholism	11.5
		hyperactive child	7.7
Ethnicity		brain damage	3.8
white	81.9	suicidal	19.2
African American	9.6	borderline personality	3.8
Hispanic	7.2	unspecified problem	3.8
Native American	1.2	psychotic outburst	3.8
Marital History		*Felony Arrest Record*	
never married	53.7	multiple arrests	63.4
married once	36.6	arson	23.9
multiple marriages	9.7	aggravated assault	1.4
		burglary	2.8
Education: Highest Grade Completed		grand theft auto	1.4
3	1.3	DWI	1.4
4	2.7	robbery	1.4
5	2.7	attempted arson	1.4
6	6.7	child molestation	2.8
7	1.3		

TABLE 7.3 Continued

Method of Apprehension			alone	16.3
turned self in or confessed	21.1		female roommate	4.7
informant	7.0		male roommate	7.0
witness	12.7		both sex roommates	2.3
key evidence recovered	4.2		spouse	2.3
law enforcement investigation	38.0		spouse and children	4.7
caught in act	9.9		grandparents	7.0
arson while in jail	4.2		institution	14.0
caught fleeing the scene	1.4		mixed	18.5
multiple events	1.4			
			Type of Residence	
Plea Offered			rooming house	18.1
guilty	52.6		hotel/motel	2.4
not guilty	28.9		apartment	23.8
changed to guilty	10.5		single-family house	42.9
combination	7.9		institution	11.9
Area/Time Arson Committed			*Method of Selection*	
work/school	2.5		knew the people at target site	2.9
to/from work/school	7.5		worked at target site	5.9
after work hours	42.5		random selection	17.6
days off/weekends	10.0		walking distance	5.9
multiple locations	12.5			
home or other	25.0		*Means of Gaining Access*	
			open entry	37.8
Distance From Home to Arson Site			broke in	18.9
0-1 block	2.7		had a key	2.7
1-2 blocks	5.4		lived there	10.8
2-5 blocks	12.2		set outside	13.5
½ to 1 mile	29.7		multiple means	16.2
1-2 miles	20.3			
2-5 miles	4.1		*Ignition Device*	
5-10 miles	5.4		wooden matches	7.9
10-20 miles	2.7		book matches	57.9
20-40 miles	2.7		cigarette lighter	17.1
varied distances	6.8		combination	6.6
home/institution	6.8		Molotov cocktail	2.6
			cigarette	2.6
Mode of Transportation to Scene			road flare	1.3
walking	60.8		candle	1.3
bicycle	5.1		gunpowder	1.3
motorcycle	2.5			
automobile	16.5		*Items Left at Scene*	
truck	1.3		gas can	13.9
already at scene	7.6		matches	47.2
mixed modes	6.3		cigarette lighter	5.6
			other devices	11.1
Living Arrangements at Time of Arson			multiple items	25.0
parents	23.3			

SOURCE: Sapp et al. (n.d.).
NOTE: This information is from a government document and is in the public domain.

considered by many to be motiveless. Pyromaniacs have been described as: " . . . offenders who said they set their fires for no practical reason and received no material profit from the act, their only motive being to obtain some sort of sensual satisfaction" (Lewis and Yarnell, 1951: 42).

Lewis and Yarnell in their study found that the pyromaniac represented 60 percent of their sample population. Of this number, 241 expressed receiving some sort of satisfaction from the fire. The remaining 447 offenders "offered no special reason or persistent interest beyond the fact that something within them forced them to set fires" (Ibid., 86).

This urge to set fires has been referred to as the "irresistible impulse." However, authorities should be cautioned on accepting this explanation.

Some researchers have postulated that this behavior is the release of sexual tension. Gold agrees that sexual tension may be a motivational factor in some incendiarism but rejects it as a major causative factor, and Lewis and Yarnell found only a small percentage who claimed to have received some sort of sexual gratification from their firesetting. (Gold, 1962: 407)

In their *Crime Classification Manual,* Douglas et al. (1992) identify three types of arson: serial arson, spree arson, and mass arson. The *serial arsonist* is "involved in three or more separate firesetting episodes, with a characteristic emotional cooling-off period between fires" (pp. 186-187). This definition is similar to the definition of serial murder we have stated earlier in this book. As Icove (1990) notes, "This form of firesetting is most serious due to the unique selection of victims and unpredictable gaps between incidents" (p. 47).

The *spree arsonist* "sets fires at three or more separate locations with no emotional cooling-off period between them" (Douglas et al., 1992, p. 189). The *mass arsonist* is "one person who sets three or more fires at the same location during a limited period of time" (p. 189).

In addition to defining the various forms of arson, Douglas et al. have developed a typology of arsonists that suggests certain social core and behavioral variables and traits that may be common to different types of arsonists; these characteristics can have important

Characteristics of Pyromaniacs

Age: Heaviest concentration between ages of 16-28; highest frequency at age 17.

Sex: Male.

Race: Predominantly white.

Intelligence: Ranges from mentally defective to genius (approximately 22% of those with no explanation for their fire setting are low-grade defectives).

Physical defects: Frequently found to be present.

Enuresis: Present in some.

Mental disorders: Psychopathy, as well as psychotic disorders, have been identified within this category; the compulsive urge also appears to reflect a neurotic obsessive-compulsive pattern of behavior.

Academic adjustment: Poor educational adjustment, although some pyromaniacs are intellectually bright. Their academic performance is marginal or scholastically retarded—underachievers.

Rearing environment: Pathological, broken, and harsh rearing environment with inconsistent discipline and parental neglect. Pyromaniacs note unhappy home life.

Social class structure: Some pyromaniacs emerge from middle-class or even upper socioeconomic levels; others are products of lower-class environments.

Social adjustment: Socially maladjusted, severe problems in developing and maintaining interpersonal relationships.

Marital adjustment: Although some pyromaniacs are married, their marital adjustments are poor.

Sexual adjustment: Sexually maladjusted and inadequate; limited contact with women.

Occupational/employment history: Most frequently unskilled laborers, if employed. They accept subservient positions and become resentful when they realize their work is degrading.

continued

Personality: May be described as misfits and feeble persons, physical cowards with feelings of inadequacy, inferiority, insufficiency, and self-consciousness; introverted, reclusive, aloof, frustrated, and lonely. Often pyromaniacs have unconscious fears of being unwanted and unloved and suffer from wounded self-esteem and lack of pride and prestige. They often project an image of calm and indifference (anxiety and tension are present nonetheless). They have vague feelings, however, that their defenses will fail them and that these repressed impulses will emerge. They tend to be defensive and obstinate in attitude and ambivalent toward authority. Although they have an inner dependency on authority, they also have contempt for authority. In fact, they have repressed their rage and hatred toward society and authority figures. They lack ambition and aggressiveness. Some state that they had no desire to hurt anyone. They may be apologetic, but ashamed for being apologetic. They seek expression through excitement. Some pyromaniacs have been found to be quite intelligent, neat, and methodical in their behavior. They have a need to be recognized and have a sense of worth. They have a craving for power and prestige. They fail to express remorse or to accept responsibility for their fire-setting behavior.

Criminal history: Many have histories of delinquency and criminal behavior, including runaway, burglary, theft, and other property offenses.

Use of alcohol: Pyromaniacs frequently use alcohol as a method of escape and to remove social inhibitions, but they do not set fires because they drink.

Suicide: Some attempt suicide after arrest and incarceration.

Motives: Exact motivation in each case is unknown, but the following motives have been identified: (a) desire to be a hero and center of attention (craving for excitement and prestige)—playing detective at the fire, rendering first aid, helping to rescue victims, assisting firefighters; (b) desire to show themselves sufficiently clever to cause the "experts" (firefighters and detectives) problems and to render them helpless—grandiose ambitions to be the executive who directs the firefighting activity and puts the firefighters into action; (c) enjoyment of the destruction of property (vagrants exhibiting pyromania receive sadistic pleasure in watching the destruction of buildings); (d) irresistible impulse (unable to offer any other explanation); (e) revenge, although not consciously present, a possible factor; (f) sexual satisfaction (noted in a relatively small percentage of cases).

Irresistible impulse: No single precipitating factor produces this impulse. It is believed to be the result of an accumulation of problems that cause stress, frustration, and tension. Examples include thwarted sexual desires, loss of employment, refusal of employment, death of parent or loved one, threats to personal security and masculinity, explosive protest over imagined immorality or promiscuousness of mother or spouse, and fear of impotence.

Types of fires: Generally made in haste and in a disorganized fashion; often set in rubbish, basements, and in and around inhabited dwellings, office buildings, schools, hotels, and other structures in thickly populated sections of cities. Fires frequently set in rapid succession. Matches, newspapers, and other available materials are used in starting the fires.

Number of fires: May start numerous fires, sometimes hundreds, until caught.

False alarms: Some pyromaniacs also make false alarms.

Time of day: Fire setting is often nocturnal.

Regard for life: No regard for life exhibited; fires are frequently set in and around occupied buildings.

Emotional state and behavior during fire setting: Many feel the act of fire setting is outside themselves; some describe the emergence of a sort of dissociative state (a transient sensation of being controlled by an external force—a feeling of being automated). They recognize the fire setting is senseless but do not have the control to prevent it. To a casual observer, the pyromaniac appears normal.

continued

Emotional state and behavior after fire setting: Relief and even exaltation; tensions released. Few express sexual satisfaction in setting fires. Many often stay at or near the fire as a spectator, or to assist responding firefighters by rendering first aid or rescuing victims. Some enjoy playing detective at the fire scene. Some, after setting a fire and ensuring firefighters' response, go home to a restful sleep.

Arrest: Some pyromaniacs ensure that they will be identified and arrested; some even turned themselves in to the police. Many continue to set fires until apprehended. For some, arrest seems to release them from their irresistible impulses to set fires. It is a relief for them to be stopped.

Confession: Many readily confess or admit guilt, though they express no remorse or regret for their behavior; neither do they generally accept responsibility for their fire-setting activity. They are most often quiet and cooperative under arrest.

Selection of target: Fire-setting targets are often randomly selected, for no apparent reason.

Recidivism: Rate of recidivism has been found to be 28%.

SOURCE: Adapted from Lewis and Yarnell (1951, p. 42) by Rider (1980a, pp. 14-15).

---

implications for crime scene assessment. Douglas et al. (1992) divide arsonists into six categories: those who commit arson for vandalism, for excitement, for revenge, and for profit, those commit arson to conceal other crimes, and extremists. We discuss the first five of these types below.

ARSON FOR VANDALISM

Vandalizing arsonists tend to be relatively young and often will act in groups. The typical target is an educational facility, but these arsonists will sometimes select residential areas or areas of dense vegetation. These arsonists often come from a lower-class background, live close to where they commit their crimes (usually within a mile), and live at home with their parents. Usually these offenders are not abusers of drugs or alcohol, at least during the same period when they set fires. In addition, sexual excitement is not a motivating factor or a factor in their choice of targets. These arsonists generally set fires on weekday afternoons and on weekends, times that correspond with periods when school is not in session, as many of this group are of junior high to high school age. As we have noted, 49% of all arson fires are set by young people, and the majority of these are between the ages of 10 and 14.

After the vandal arson sets a fire, he will usually flee the scene and not return. If he does return, he generally watches the scene from a safe distance.

ARSON FOR EXCITEMENT

Douglas et al. (1992) name as subtypes of the excitement arsonist the thrill seeker, the attention seeker, the recognition seeker, and the sexually perverted. The excitement arsonist craves attention and finds that setting fires is one way to gain it. He will set fires and watch the activity from a guarded distance. If he remains close to the scene, he will try to blend in with other bystanders.

The targets for the excitement fire setter include vegetation, large trash receptacles, and construction sites, as well as residential areas. This arsonist tends to use rather simple incendiary materials, such as matches or cigarettes, but in our experience we have also found that older offenders of this type may use more complex fire-setting devices, such as time-delay mechanisms. The setting of multiple fires may be associated with the arsonist's progressive learning about and use of more complex devices. Unlike the vandal fire setter, this arsonist tends to come from a middle-class family and to live with both parents.

This type of offender often has an arrest record, and the older the offender, the longer the arrest history. He will typically commit his crimes alone, but may on occasion commit arson in the company of one other person. As with the vandal arsonist, sexual gratification does not generally play an important role in the arsonist's motivation, although some of these kinds of fire setters have attached a sexual component to the excitement they hope to stimulate by starting fires. Investigators should be alert to the possible presence at the scene of sexual paraphernalia, such as pornography, and evidence of sexual activity, such as semen.

ARSON FOR REVENGE

The revenge arsonist sets fires with the goal of gaining revenge for a real or imagined injury. This arsonist may be quite different from other arsonists, especially those who could be termed serial arsonists. The fire setting of this kind of arsonist is likely to be a one-time occurrence centered on the destruction of a particular dwelling, business, or facility connected to someone the offender believes has done him or her an injustice. This attack may be focused on an individual, a business (e.g., a former employer's workplace), a government facility, or a group of persons, such as a rival gang. This arsonist usually comes from a lower-class background and has a higher level of education than the vandal or excitement arsonist, having completed more than 10 years of formal education.

When women are arsonists, they tend to be of the revenge type. A woman who sets fires for revenge may burn items that belong to a former lover or husband, such as the person's clothing or other personal possessions. For male revenge arsonists, the typical targets are residential and business property units.

Revenge arsonists often commit their crimes on weekends, in the afternoon, evening, or early morning hours, and often at locations within a 1-mile radius of their homes. They do not tend to stay at their crime scenes because they want to distance themselves from the fires they set; they also seldom return to the scenes of their crimes. Unlike vandal and excitement arsonists, these fire setters often use alcohol as a means of lowering their inhibitions before they commit their crimes.

Sexual gratification is not usually a motivating factor for the revenge arsonist. The precipitating factor in this form of arson is a personal affront to the offender, whether real or imagined. It should be noted that sometimes the affront occurs several months or even years before the arsonist decides to take revenge by setting a fire.

ARSON FOR CRIME CONCEALMENT

Arson committed to conceal another crime—by destroying evidence or by misleading authorities—is clearly secondary to the commission of that other crime. For example, in one case of a fire set to conceal a murder, a man killed his wife, decapitated her, buried her head in the rear yard, and then burned the woman's corpse inside the house. In this case, the arson failed to conceal the crime. When the fire department responded to the house fire, the firefighters discovered the headless body and notified the police, who found the head buried in the rear yard.

Many arson fires set to conceal other crimes involve an abundance of liquid accelerant, but often because of the incompetence of the fire setter, evidence of the original crime is not totally destroyed. Ressler, Burgess, and Douglas (1988) note that this form of crime scene tends to be of the disorganized variety; consequently, there is apt to be more physical evidence at the scene than would be the case if it were of the organized type.

The arsonist who acts to conceal another crime is likely to be an adult male from a lower-class background who lives alone. He tends to live slightly farther away from his crime scenes than the other types of arsonists described so far, and often commits his crimes in the company of another person. He tends to commit his crimes in the evening or in the early morning hours, and will flee the crime scene once the fire has started.

As with most of the kinds of fire setters mentioned so far, sexual gratification is not a primary motivating factor for this arsonist. His goal is simple and utilitarian: to get rid of the evidence of a crime that has already occurred, whether a homicide, burglary, vehicle theft, or something else. If the primary crime is a murder, this arsonist is usually not a serial arsonist, as usually for this type of person the crime of homicide is a one-time occurrence. If this is the case, the fire setter usually acts alone. However, if the fire is set to hide a crime other than murder, it may be the work of a serial arsonist, and he will usually be accompanied by another person when he sets the fire.

Alcohol, and possibly other drugs, plays an important role in the commission of this kind of arson by lessening the inhibitions of the fire setter and enabling the perpetration of the crime.

Douglas et al. (1992) offer no information concerning the education level, employment status, or arrest record of this form of fire setter, but it may be inferred that, like the other arsonists described above, he has a limited level of education. Further, if he is employed, he likely works at a menial job that requires little education, and he may have a long history of involvement with the criminal justice system, because crimes such as burglary and robbery are common serial crimes. In addition, almost four out of five of this type of arsonist are single.

ARSON FOR PROFIT

The least passionate arsonist is the adult male who sets fires for material gain. Sometimes this fire setter is hired by a failing business owner who wishes to collect insurance monies, deplete inventory, or the like. This kind of arsonist tends to set fires after business hours, in the evening or early morning. This arsonist has no motive to cover up another crime, no sexual motive, and no revenge motive; he sets fires solely for material gain. Such a person may be hired by others to commit this crime, and so may be a serial arsonist.

This kind of fire setter tends to be a single man who lives alone, usually more than a mile from the scenes of the fires he sets, to which he travels in some kind of vehicle. By the time the fire or explosion he has set occurs, he may be far away from the scene. He may have an accomplice who assists him in setting up fires, and this second person may be in the position of an apprentice.

The experience this kind of arsonist has with the criminal justice system may be quite extensive. He may have an arrest record in robbery, burglary, public disorderly conduct, and public drunken-

TABLE 7.4 Social and Behavioral Characteristics of Five Types of Arsonists

| Characteristics | Type of Arsonist | | | | |
	Vandalism	Excitement	Revenge	Crime Concealment	Profit
Age	juvenile	juvenile	adult	adult	adult
Social class	lower to middle class	middle class	lower class	lower class	working class
Time of crime	afternoon	afternoon, evening	afternoon, evening, early morning	evening, early morning	evening, morning
Day of crime	weekdays	varies	weekends	varies	weekdays
Lives with	parents	alone	alone	alone	alone
Alcohol or drug use	no	no	yes	yes	yes
Proximity to crime	<1 mile	<1 mile	<1 mile	>1 mile	>1 mile
Committed crime alone	no	yes	yes	no	no
Remains at crime scene	yes	yes	no	no	no
Sex motive	no	no	no	no	no
Education	grades 6-8	grade 10	grades 10+	<high school	<high school
Employment	no	no	yes	yes	no
Arrest record	juvenile	yes	yes	yes	yes
Marital status	single	single	single	single	single

SOURCES: Data are from Douglas et al. (1992) and Sapp et al. (n.d.).

ness. In addition, as this man may be a serial arsonist, as noted above, he may have an arrest record as an arsonist.

Douglas et al. (1992) note that this type of fire setter is usually 25 to 40 years old and has less than a high school education. This is a crime of premeditation, which suggests that the arsonist is at least of average intelligence, so it is likely that his lack of academic performance rests with outside forces rather than intellectual abilities. The crime scene associated with this kind of arsonist is an organized one.

Of course, investigators should approach every crime with the knowledge that the perpetrator is a unique individual, but it is a basic and useful assumption of psychological profiling that the crime

TABLE 7.5 Search Warrant Suggestions for Five Types of Arsonists

Vandalism
  Spray paint can
  Items from the scene, especially if a school was the target
  Explosive devices: fireworks, firecrackers, packaging, or cartons
  Flammable liquids
  Clothing: evidence of flammable liquid, evidence of glass particles, for witness
    identification
  Shoes: footprints, flammable liquid traces

Excitement
  Vehicle
    Material similar to incendiary devices used: fireworks, containers that components
      were shipped in; packaging, wires, etc.
    Floor mats, trunk padding, carpeting: residue from accelerants (not conclusive
      evidence, but indicative)
    Beer cans, matchbooks, cigarettes, to match any brands found at the scene
  House
    Material similar to incendiary devices used: fireworks, containers that components
      were shipped in, packages, wires, etc.
    Clothing, shoes: accelerant and soil samples if vegetation fire
    Cigarette lighter, especially if subject does not smoke
    Diaries, journals, notes, logs, recordings, and maps documenting fires
    Newspapers, articles reporting fires
    Souvenirs from the crime scene

Revenge
  If accelerants used: shoes, socks, clothing, glass particles in clothing (if break-in)
  Discarded, concealed clothing
  Bottles, flammable liquids, matchbooks
  Cloth (fiber comparison), tape (if device used)
  Clothing, shoes if liquid accelerant used (or homicide victim's blood, glass fragments of
    windows broken during burglary attempt)

Crime concealment
  Refer to category dealing with primary motive
  Gasoline containers
  Clothing, shoes if liquid accelerant used (or if homicide victim's blood)
  Glass fragments if windows broken during burglary attempt
  Burned paper documents

Profit
  Check financial records
  If evidence of fuel/air explosion at the scene, check emergency room for patients with
    burn injuries
  Determine condition of utilities (gas, electric) as soon as possible (eliminate gas, the
    common accidental cause of fires)

SOURCE: Adapted from Douglas et al. (1992).

scene reflects the personality of the offender. The above discussion of the characteristics of arsonists and the following discussion of the categories of organized and disorganized personality as applied to arsonists are intended to give potential profilers some guidance about what to look for in arson crime scenes.

ORGANIZED VERSUS DISORGANIZED PERSONALITY IN THE ARSONIST

Some of the characteristics of arsonists discussed above have important implications regarding organization or lack of organization at the arson crime scene. As we have noted, some kinds of arsonists tend to be better organized than others; this can be useful information for the profiler, because some of the observations we have made in preceding chapters regarding organized and disorganized offenders may be applied to arsonists.

The profiler might also keep in mind the model of personal violence discussed in Chapter 6, and be alert to social or personal events that may send an arsonist into the fall from the stage of distorted thinking, especially if the crime is committed for motives intrinsic to the personality of the offender. That is, some arsonists may respond to negative experiences by setting fires to regain their sense of self-importance.

According to Douglas et al. (1992, p. 166), organized and disorganized arson crime scenes tend to display certain elements. Organized arsonists are associated with the following:

- Elaborate incendiary devices (electronic timing mechanisms, initiators, and so on)
- Relative lack of physical evidence, compared with disorganized arsonists; more skillful forced entry if any (lack of footprints, fingerprints, and so on)
- Methodical approach (trailers, multiple sets, excessive accelerant use, and so on)

In contrast, disorganized arsonists are associated with these elements:

- Use of materials that happened to be on hand
- Matches, cigarettes, and common accelerants (lighter fluid, gasoline)
- More physical evidence left (handwriting, footprints, fingerprints, and the like)

These lists illustrate our argument that the personality of the offender is reflected in the nature of the crime scene. The more disorganization within the offender's personality, the more disorganized the crime scene. This point is well illustrated in the writings of Rider (1980a, 1980b), Sapp et al. (n.d.), and Douglas et al. (1992).

CONCLUSION

The crime of arson costs U.S. society millions of dollars each year, not to mention the cost in human lives. An initial step in the investigation of arson is to come to some understanding about the kinds of persons who commit this crime. Just as there are different types of arson, there are different kinds of arsonists; the personalities of those who set fires are varied. An assessment of the arson crime scene and what it can reveal about the particular arsonist is the first step toward the successful solution of crime.

NOTE

1. The discussion in this chapter relies in great part on the work of Douglas et al. (1992) and Sapp et al. (n.d.), to whom we are indebted.

8. Psychological Profiling and Rape

Rape is a crime that has definite cultural definitions. Brownmiller (1975) asserts that rape is "a conscious process of intimidation by which all men keep all women in a state of fear" (p. 115). She further adds that rape in time of war has long been considered the victor's prerogative; the vanquished surrender yet another form of property. When women are viewed as chattel, rape confirms their inferior social position. Conversely, a study of rape in Pennsylvania conducted in the early 1970s espoused a position of victim precipitation (Amir, 1971). This stance "validated" many of the myths about rape: Women secretly want to be raped, the primary motive for rape is sex, and so on. In this chapter, we focus on the roles of sex and power in the repugnant crime of rape. We do not have space available here to refute the above-mentioned myths about rape, but we want to stress that rape is a crime of power and violence in which sex is the weapon.

DEFINITIONS OF RAPE

Rape may be defined as the crime of having sexual intercourse with another person forcibly and against his or her will (Kenney & More, 1994, p. 33). Rape is often viewed, mistakenly, as a sexually motivated act; in reality, it is a violent crime. *Statutory rape* is sexual intercourse that is unlawful because it involves a person younger than the age prescribed by statute as the age of consent (Bennett & Hess, 1994, p. 361). *Forcible rape* is sexual penetration without a person's consent; this is the crime with which we are concerned in this chapter.

Although in this chapter we address primarily what may be called "stranger rape," it should be noted that in recent years the very character of what is viewed as rape has been changing, as the phenomenon of "date rape" or "acquaintance rape" has received a great deal of attention. In some ways, our cultural view of what constitutes rape may be shifting (Gibbs, 1991). Only with time will we gain improved perspective on this form of sexual crime (Dunham & Alpert, 1993, p. 91).

STATISTICS ON RAPE

According to FBI estimates, almost 132,000 rapes were reported in the United States in 1992 (U.S. Department of Justice, FBI, 1993, p. 249). This figure does not include, of course, rapes that were unreported. Many researchers believe that a great many rapes are not reported, for a number of reasons, including victims' feelings of shame, victims' beliefs that police will not believe them, victims' fear of reprisals, and victims' lack of faith in the criminal justice system (Palmiotto, 1994, pp. 253, 261). Whatever the reasons, vic-timization reports suggest higher rates of rape than the FBI data show (see U.S. Department of Justice, 1991, p. 6).

Men, too, are sometimes victims of rape, but it is clear that men are raped at much lower rates than are women. One study suggests that males account for 1% of all reported rape victims (Groth &

Burgess, 1980, p. 806), and Glick (1995, p. 207) reports that, of 141,000 rapes reported in 1992, males were victims in about 8% of the cases. (Of course, these statistics do not include men who are raped in prisons.)

The majority of rape victims are young, with those in the age cohort of 16-24 being two to three times more likely than those in other age groups to become victims. Most rape victims are white, but black females are disproportionally represented among victims in comparison with their numbers in the general population. Rape victims also tend to be single and from the lower socioeconomic class (Schwendinger & Schwendinger, 1983; U.S. Department of Justice, 1988).

Marital rape, which we will not address further in this book, is undoubtedly underreported. Russell (1982) estimates that one husband in seven, on at least one occasion, sexually forces his wife to submit to coitus, oral sex, or anal sex.

Attempted but uncompleted stranger rape typically occurs on the street, in a park or playground, or in a parking lot or parking garage during daylight hours. Completed stranger rape most often occurs in the victim's home in the period from 6:00 p.m. to midnight (U.S. Department of Justice, 1988).

Rape statistics may be very misleading, given that some researchers believe that less than 10% of all rapes are reported. As noted above, there are many reasons for women's reluctance to report having been raped. Especially before rape "shield laws" were in place, women often feared that their own sexual backgrounds could be made an issue during the prosecution of a rape case. Indeed, many rape victims have been subjected to yet another vicious personal attack in the courtroom at the hands of defense attorneys. Perhaps the paramount reason many women are reluctant to report rape is the stigma that is still attached to the status of rape victim; in our society it is still common for members of the public to blame the victim, to believe that the victim somehow invited the attack or cooperated with the rapist.

Of course, every rape should be reported. In recent years there have been some improvements in the rates of reporting, in part because of changes in the laws in many states that have effectively limited the right of accused rapists' defense attorneys to introduce in court the victims' sexual histories, and in part owing to increased sensitivity within law enforcement and improved evidence gathering methods in cases of alleged rape, perhaps a side effect of the increase in the number of female police officers on many police forces.

There are those who believe that some women make false accusations of rape as a form of revenge against men they wish to punish, but it appears that although this occurs, it is very infrequent. One recent study found that only approximately 15% of all accusations of rape are unfounded (Palmiotto, 1994, p. 262).

SELECTED CHARACTERISTICS OF RAPISTS

A cursory examination of the research conducted on rapists in cases of stranger rape yields some general information. For example, rapists tend to be young, with 80% under the age of 30 and 75% under the age of 25 (Kelley, 1976; Queen's Bench Foundation, 1976). Many come from lower-class backgrounds and are members of minority groups (often black); most choose victims of their own race (Hagan, 1986, p. 185; Hazelwood & Warren, 1989). Many rapists' psychosexual backgrounds include histories of conflict and other trouble with women, as well as marked inability to relate to women personally and sexually (Queen's Bench Foundation, 1976, p. 189). Rapists are usually unarmed; in the one case in four when a rapist is armed, the weapon is usually a knife or other sharp instrument (Glick, 1995, p. 206; U.S. Department of Justice, 1988). Most stranger rapists plan their attacks (Amir, 1971), and most have histories of violence. One in three has a prior record for a violent crime, and 25% have been before the court for rape (Queen's Bench Foundation, 1976).

It should be emphasized that the above characteristics apply only to perpetrators of stranger rape. A growing amount of data suggest that date or acquaintance rape may be much more common than stranger rape (Dr. Richard Tewksberry, personal communication, March 28, 1995), but that is a topic that is beyond the scope of this volume. We are concerned here with the violent personal crime of rape as perpetrated by rapists who have not had previous relationships with their victims.

PSYCHOLOGY AND RAPE

If we assume that rape is a crime of violence in which sex is the weapon, we can see that certain psychological elements may be expected to be present, elements similar to those found in other violent personal offenses. In addition to these elements, rapists appear to have three added dimensions to their pattern of violent behavior: power, anger, and sexuality (Groth, Burgess, & Holmstrom, 1977). Further, the following intrapersonal variables have been associated with the rapist personality: deficiencies in heterosocial skill development and abuse of alcohol and/or other psychoactive substances as biochemical lubricants, such as exposure to violent pornography (Pallone & Hennessy, 1992, pp. 246-247; see also Linz, 1989).

The elements of power and anger in rape, combined with the crime's sexual component, lend themselves well to psychological profiling. The investigator will find many factors suitable to the examination and interpretation of a personality that insists upon a violent personal attack, sometimes fatal, to find a release from tension and compulsion (Holmes, 1995).

There is no simple way to explain why anyone becomes a rapist. Certainly, not all rapists are alike, and rapists' motives, anticipations, and expectations vary. There has been a great deal of interest shown by researchers regarding the effects of early childhood interaction and later personality development of the rapist in which the relationship between the mother and the rapist has been the major focus. The rapist's relationship with his father has been considered to be less significant. The mother of the rapist is usually described as having been, in the rapist's childhood, rejecting, excessively controlling, dominant, punitive, overprotective, and seductive. The father is usually described as uninvolved, aloof, distant, absent, or passive, but occasionally punitive and cruel. Some researchers suggest that in the case of the sex offender, parental cruelty, inconsistency of discipline, envy, and sexual frustration, as well as overstimulation or seduction, are the principal factors that influence the rapist's sexual personality and criminal behavior (Holmes, 1983; Rada, 1978).

The rapist may have experienced parental seductiveness in childhood, usually from his mother; this may have ranged from covert seductive behaviors to actual sexual involvement. There may be a history of early prolonged bed sharing with a sibling or parent that may have sensitized the rapist unduly to sexual stimulation during childhood. In some cases, rapists have shared beds with their mothers into puberty. Many rapists also have a history of severe physical punishment by dominating, sadistic, and castrating mothers. Their fathers, if present, may not have lent needed support to their children when it was needed. Thus, a rapist's hostility toward women in general in adulthood may stem from the pain he suffered at the hands of a particular woman, his mother.

In summary, the professional literature suggests that parental rejection, domination, cruelty, and seductiveness are important factors in the early life of the rapist. During childhood, mild to moderate social maladjustments of the future rapist may be evidenced in fighting, temper tantrums, truancy, and stealing.

Regardless of their etiology, rapists are perceived somewhat differently by men and women in our society. Sanders (1983) points out that many men tend to look down on rapists as less than fully masculine:

In effect, they "hit girls" and that is something only wimps and sissies do. This conceptualization of rapists is less flattering than that of their being truly "violent men"—men to be taken seriously, dangerous men not to be trifled with. It is also a good reputation for rapists since it scares the victims into submission. However, it is inaccurate. The greater the resistance of women in rapes, the more likely rapists will run off. In the world of violent men, rapists are considered punks and generally low life. . . . Thus, while rapists loom large as fiends and overpowering monsters to women, they loom small to men, more mice than men. (p. 73)

A study of violent rapists being treated at the Atascadero State Hospital in California reported the following (Queen's Bench Foundation, 1976):

1. The majority of the rapists demonstrated poor relations with women, lack of self-confidence, and negative self-concepts.
2. Of the sample, 51% indicated they were seeking power or dominance over their victims.
3. The majority had planned to have sex on the day they committed rape, and 92% said rape was their intention.
4. None of the 75 subjects indicated a lack of sexual outlet as a reason for his crime.

TYPOLOGY OF RAPISTS

Many researchers have attempted to classify various kinds of rapists (Amir, 1971; Becker & Abel, 1978; Cohen, Garofalo, Boucher, & Seghorn, 1971; Douglas, Burgess, Burgess, & Ressler, 1992; Knight, Carter, & Prentky, 1989; Knight & Prentky, 1987). The FBI's Behavioral Science Unit has been somewhat successful in its attempt to offer a typology, and Groth et al. (1977) have designed a taxonomy predicated on the elements of power, rage, and sex. In an especially useful study for our purposes here, Knight and Prentky (1987) offer a typology that divides rapists into four categories: power reassurance, anger retaliation, exploitive, and sadistic (see also Bradway, 1990; Douglas et al., 1992).

POWER REASSURANCE RAPIST

Power reassurance rapists, also termed *compensatory rapists,* are the least violent and aggressive of the four types. They are also the least socially competent, suffering from extremely low self-esteem and feelings of inadequacy.

The backgrounds of such rapists vary. Knight and Prentky (1987) report that the overwhelming majority (88%) are from homes where either mother or father was present. Many have had minor problems in school, and their average education level is tenth grade. The compensatory rapist is most often single and lives with one or both of his parents. He is nonathletic, quiet, and passive; he has few friends and no sex partner. Often he lives in a home where he is dominated by an aggressive and possibly seductive mother. He may spend some time frequenting adult bookstores in his own neighborhood. Because of his limited education level, he is often employed in some type of menial occupation and is viewed as a steady, reliable worker.

The power reassurance rapist may have a variety of sexual aberrations. He may be involved in transvestism, for example, or in promiscuous sexual behavior, exhibitionism, voyeurism, fetishism, or excessive masturbation (Shook, 1990). The possible voyeurism of such rapists is an important element for profilers to keep in mind, as it may lead these rapists to select victims in their own immediate neighborhoods (Kenney & More, 1994). For example, one such rapist with more than a score of victims reportedly stalked his victims by looking in their bedroom windows and then entering their houses through those windows when the opportunities arose (G. Barret, personal communication, 1995).

Table 8.1 lists the social core variables of the power reassurance rapist. Of course, the variables shown in this table and the others in this chapter are meant as general guidelines; they will not fit perfectly every rapist who may be categorized as a particular type (Knight & Prentky, 1987).

Elements in the rape process. The basic purpose of rape for the power reassurance rapist is to elevate his own self-status. The primary aim is sexual, in contrast to the generally accepted notion that rape is not primarily a sexual behavior but a means of assault in which sex is secondary. For this rapist, the sex act validates his

TABLE 8.1 Social Characteristics of the Power Reassurance Rapist

Single	Menial occupation
Lives with parents	Frequents adult bookstores
No sex partner	Voyeur
Nonathletic	Exhibitionist
Quiet, passive	Transvestite
Social loner	Fetishist

TABLE 8.2 Elements in the Power Reassurance Rape

Neighborhood attack	Rapist travels on foot
Rapist believes victim enjoys the rape	Rapist may be impotent
Little use of profanity	Use of weapons of opportunity
Rapist wants victim to "talk dirty"	Increasing violence during rape
Victim asked to remove clothing	Possible later contact of victims
Only body parts essential for the rape to occur are exposed	Possible covering of victim's face
Victim of rapist's age cohort	Rapes continue until rapist apprehended
Victim of rapist's race	Possible collection of souvenirs
Rape committed every 7-15 days	Possible keeping of diary by rapist

position of importance. He perceives himself as a loser, and by controlling another human being he hopes to make himself believe that he is important, if only temporarily. For this reason, he uses only enough force to control his victim.

This kind of rapist's behavior during the commission of his crime is an expression of his sexual fantasies. For this reason, he is concerned with the physical welfare of his victim and will not usually harm her intentionally. He operates under the assumption that his victim actually enjoys the rape. He may request that his victim "talk dirty" to him, but he will use little profanity himself in his verbal exchanges with his victim. He may politely ask his victim to remove her clothing, and will often expose only the body parts necessary for the rape to occur (see Table 8.2).

The power reassurance rapist tends to choose victims from his own age cohort and within his own race, and he usually rapes within his own neighborhood or close to his place of employment, because he travels on foot. He generally commits his rapes at night, in the period from midnight to 5:00 a.m. The time between rapes for this offender tends to be from 7 to 15 days. Although his rapes generally begin with relatively little violence, the violence may increase as an attack continues. He will choose a weapon, if he needs one, from the home of his victim. He may also collect souvenirs from victim's home.

The power reassurance rapist is the only one of the four types of rapists described here who may later contact his victims to inquire about their health, as though he is concerned about the possible ill effects of the rape. This kind of rapist may also be so convinced that his victims enjoyed being raped that he may promise to return. In one case we know of, such a rapist promised to return the next day, and when he did, the police were waiting for him.

This kind of rapist may have some kind of sexual dysfunction, such as impotence. In addition, he may keep a diary in which he keeps track of the names of his victims and describes his rapes.

Interviewing strategy. Like most kinds of rapists, the power reassurance rapist will continue raping until he is caught. Unfortunately, there is no clear-cut best strategy to use in interrogating this type of offender once he has been apprehended. The interviewer should be aware of the basic reason behind this offender's crimes: By raping, he seeks to resolve his self-doubts; he has no real intent to inflict harm on others. Because of this, one strategy that may be useful in interviewing is to appeal to his sense of masculinity. The interviewer might indicate to him that the woman who has been raped in the case under investigation has not suffered "undue" trauma, and that the police realize the rapist had no desire to harm his victim; such a statement could set the stage for a "sympathetic" relationship that might result in the rapist's sharing information, not only about the rape currently under investigation, but about other suspected connected rapes.

Because this kind of offender wants to be understood and not condemned, another possible strategy is for the interviewer to appear to empathize with the suspect, assuming the role of a "father confessor."

TABLE 8.3 Social Characteristics of the Anger Retaliation Rapist

Parents divorced	20% adopted
Ninth-grade education	Does not assault wife
Married	Athletic
Majority physically abusive (56%)	Frequents bars
Socially competent	Likes contact sports
Hates women	Action-oriented occupations

TABLE 8.4 Elements in the Anger Retaliation Rape

Neighborhood attack	Rapes committed every 6 months to a year
Blitz attack	
Little planning	Possible ejaculation into the face of the victim
Intent to harm the victim	
Use of weapons of opportunity	Anal and oral sex
Ripping off of victim's clothing	Victim of same age as or older than rapist
Use of excessive profanity	
Situation-precipitated attack	Possible retarded ejaculation
Increasing aggression	

ANGER RETALIATION RAPIST

Unlike the power reassurance rapist, the anger retaliation rapist has as his general overarching purpose to hurt women. He wants to rape to get even with all women for the injustices, real or imaginary, he has suffered at the hands of other females in his life. As the list in Table 8.3 makes clear, this violent personal offender is usually very socially competent. Typically, the family situation from which he comes has been anything but pleasant or normal. More than half (56%) of the men in this category were physically abused during childhood by one or both of their parents. Approximately 80% come from families where the parents are divorced; further, some 20% of the men in this group of rapists were adopted children, and 53% have spent time in foster homes. Some 80% have been reared by a single female parent or other single female caregiver. Because of this rapist's experiences with his female significant others (mother, adoptive mother, foster mother, or whatever), he has adopted a position of negative and hostile feelings toward women in general.

The self-perception of this offender is very important. He sees himself as athletic and masculine, and for this reason he often seeks recreation that centers on contact sports and may also be involved in an action-oriented occupation, such as police work or race car driving. He is likely to be married and, like many rapists, is not assaultive toward his mate. Supporting his macho image, he may also be involved in a variety of extramarital affairs.

This kind of rapist's friends will often report that he has a quick, violent temper. He seems to have an uncontrollable impulse to rape, and his rapes tend to follow precipitating events involving his wife, mother, or some other significant woman in his life. This event can send him into a rage, and rape is the action that follows.

Elements in the rape process. As shown in Table 8.4, the anger retaliation rapist tends to rape close to his home. His attacks are sudden, or blitz attacks, which shows that there is little planning in his rapes. For this rapist the rape is not a sexual act; it is primarily an expression of anger. The aggression in the rape is intended to harm the victim.

The aggression manifested in the rape ranges from verbal assault to physical assault to possible murder. The rapist usually uses a great deal of profanity toward his victim, and he will often rip off her clothing and assault her with weapons of opportunity, including his fists and feet.

The anger retaliation rapist has made a vital connection between sexual gratification and his expression of anger and rage. Once he secures his victim within his "comfort zone," he uses profanity for a dual purpose: to heighten his own sexual excitement and to instill fear and terror into the victim. He feels the need to express his anger and rage in many forms. For example, this rapist may rape his victim anally and then force her to perform oral sex upon him immediately afterward. Following oral sex, he may ejaculate in her face in a further attempt to degrade her.

This type of rapist tends to seek women of his own race and in his own age group or slightly older. He stalks his victims close to his home, and he tends to travel by car. Unlike the power reassurance rapist, after this rapist commits an attack he will make no further effort to contact his victim.

Interviewing strategy. Keeping in mind this rapist's deep hatred of women, the interviewer should be male; this rapist believes that women in general have done him great injustices, and he will not cooperate with any female officer in an interview. The interview should also be conducted in a very professional and businesslike manner. One ploy that might be used is for the initial approach to the suspect to be made by a team of officers in which one is male and the other female. As this rapist will respond badly to the woman, the male officer can then suggest that the female officer leave the interviewing room. This symbolic move may convince the rapist that the male officer is the more experienced and powerful of the two, and this may influence the rapist's level of cooperation. In reference to this strategy, we have even heard it suggested, at a presentation by the Behavioral Science Unit of the FBI delivered at the Southern Police Institute, that the male officer should speak in disparaging terms about the female officer after she has left the interviewing room. We find this a rather radical position; such a strategy may be considered by many to be unethical under any circumstances.

POWER ASSERTIVE RAPIST

For the power assertive, or exploitive, rapist, rape is an attempt to express virility and personal dominance. This kind of rapist has a sense of superiority simply because he is a man, and he rapes because he believes he is entitled to—this is what men do to women.

For this offender, rape is not only a sex act, it is an impulsive act of predation. The aggression exhibited in the rape is intended to secure the compliance of the victim. The rapist is indifferent to the comfort or welfare of his victim; she is at his mercy, and she must do what he desires.

Some of the social core variables of the power assertive rapist are shown in Table 8.5. Approximately 70% of these rapists have been reared in single-parent families, and a third of them have spent time

TABLE 8.5 Social Characteristics of the Power Assertive Rapist

Raised in single-parent family (69%)	Frequents singles bars
Lived in foster homes (31%)	Macho occupation
Physically abused in childhood (74%)	Domestic problems
High school dropout	Property crime record
Serial marriages	Athletic
Image conscious	Dishonorable discharge from military

TABLE 8.6 Elements in the Power Assertive Rape

Rapist cruises singles bars	Retarded ejaculation
Attacks occur from 7:00 p.m. to 1:00 a.m.	Rapist has no further contact with victim
Victim's clothing likely to be torn	Victim conned or overpowered
20-25 days between rapes	No attempt by rapist to hide identity
Multiple assaults	Very brutal attack
Anal then oral assault	Victim of rapist's age group
Rapist selfish in behavior	Victim of rapist's race

in foster homes. Approximately 75% were victims of physical abuse during childhood (Knight & Prentky, 1987). This type of rapist generally has many domestic problems and has often been involved in a series of unhappy marriages. He is very image conscious, and tends to be a flashy dresser. He is often a regular at singles bars, and probably most of the other regulars know him as one who is always trying to pick up women, is loud and boisterous, and is continually trying to validate his image as a macho individual.

This type of offender may be involved in some type of traditionally masculine occupation, such as construction work or police work. A uniform of some kind may be part of his masculine image. He often drives a flashy car, perhaps a sports car or a particular model that is a favorite among his social crowd.

Elements in the rape process. As Table 8.6 shows, the power assertive rapist often finds his prey in singles bars, where there is always an ample supply of females from which to select.

The attack of the power assertive rapist consists of a mixture of verbal and physical violence. If resisted, he will physically overpower his victim to get what he desires. This rapist will often rip or tear the clothing off his victim—after all, he believes, she will not need them in the future, so why take care in removing them?

This type of rapist may commit multiple assaults on a particular victim, and his victims are usually of the rapist's age group. Not only will this rapist assault his victim vaginally, he will also often commit anal and then demand that she perform fellatio immediately after he withdraws. He may suffer retarded ejaculation, so he may force the victim to perform oral sex on him so that he can become physically aroused enough to rape. As noted above, for this rapist, sex is expressed as an impulsive act of predation.

The power assertive rapist tends to commit rapes in a 20- to 25-day cycle, a time span strangely similar to the length of a menstrual cycle. This contrasts with the tendency of power reassurance rapists to assault within 7- to 15-day cycles and that of anger retaliation rapists to commit new offenses approximately every 6 months to a year.

The power assertive rapist does not rape for sex, but as an act of predation. He typically has a steady sex partner, a wife or lover. This rapist feels the need to rape, and his aggression is intended to force the victim's compliance with his demands. The aggression of such rapists tends to escalate as they continue to rape. This kind of rapist may bring his own weapon to the rape situation, a behavior that shows forethought and planning.

The power assertive rapist does not hide his identity from his victims; masks, darkness, or blindfolds are not necessary. He has no intention of ever contacting his victims again.

This rapist will not apologize after the rape, nor will he collect souvenirs and/or keep a diary. He generally makes a conscious determination to rape within his own race.

Interviewing strategy. The power assertive rapist has little control over his impulses, and thus may be considered to be close to the clinical evaluation of having a character disorder. Such persons are commonly termed *sociopaths* or *psychopaths*. This kind of rapist will not respond at all well to a police interview based on assumptions or guesses. Investigators should know the details of the case and be certain of the suspect's involvement, because the power assertive rapist will appreciate a well-prepared case. If the questioning is not conducted effectively and professionally, any chance of gaining information from the rapist may be lost.

It is best for the interviewer to approach the interview session with all the facts in hand: the placement of the suspect at the scene, physical evidence that directly implicates him in the rape (or rapes), and other pertinent information that shows the interviewer is a professional. What the police should communicate is, We know you did it, and this is how we are going to prove it. If the interviewer is in error about the facts, or if there is some other reason for the rapist to discount the interviewer's competence as a professional, it is unlikely that any cooperation will be gained from the rapist through any means, including intimidation, pleas for aid, and appeals based on the victim's welfare.

SADISTIC RAPIST

Of all the types of rapists discussed here, the sadistic rapist is the most dangerous. The aim of this offender in raping is primarily the expression of his sexual-aggressive fantasies. His purpose is to inflict physical and psychological pain on his victims. Many of the rapists who fall into this category have antisocial personalities and are quite aggressive in their everyday lives, especially when criticized or thwarted in their quests for personal satisfaction. This rapist has made a vital connection between aggression and sexual gratification—in other words, he has eroticized aggression and violence.

Table 8.7 displays the social characteristics associated with the sadistic rapist. As the table shows, some 60% have been reared in single-parent homes. The majority suffered childhood physical abuse, and many come from homes where there has been evidence of sexual deviance (e.g., fathers who were rapists themselves). Many sadistic rapists have histories of such juvenile sexual pathologies as voyeurism, promiscuous sex, and excessive masturbation (Kenney & More, 1994, p. 196).

TABLE 8.7 Social Characteristics of the Sadistic Rapist

Raised in single-parent home (60%)	Some college education
Parents divorced (60%)	Married
Lived in foster homes (13%)	No arrest record
Physically abused in childhood (63%)	Age range 30-39
Raised in sexually deviant home	Compulsive personality
Middle-class family man	White-collar occupation

TABLE 8.8 Elements in the Sadistic Rape

Victim stalked	Degrading language
Victim transported	Retarded ejaculation
Use of gags, bonds, handcuffs	Increasing violence
Possible use of blindfold	Rapist has rape kit
Possible triolism	Rapist may eventually kill
Victim's clothing cut	Periods between rapes vary
Elements of ritual	Victims' ages vary

In his adult life, the typical sadistic rapist is married and is considered to be a "good family man." He often lives in a middle-class residential area where crime rates are low, is viewed as an asset to his community, has a better-than-average education, and is in a white-collar occupation.

This kind of rapist exhibits a compulsive personality, a factor that can be particularly important in the profiling process. He demonstrates his compulsiveness in his personal appearance and in the automobile he drives, which is neat, clean, and kept in good condition.

This offender is intelligent and probably does not have a police record. He has the ability to escape detection for his offenses, if for no other reason than because he carefully plans his rapes and carries them out within the parameters of his plans. His intelligence, knowledge of police work, antisocial personality, and care in the planning and implementation of his rapes make him especially difficult to apprehend.

Elements in the rape process. There is an expressive aim in the rapes of this kind of rapist. The aggression component of the rape is not simply for control; he intends to do personal harm to his victim.

If this rapist is not apprehended, he will eventually begin to kill his victims (see Table 8.8).

The sadistic rapist uses his well-maintained automobile to stalk his victims. He takes great care in selecting victims, making certain that he is not seen and taking all precautions necessary to hinder the detection of his crimes and thus his apprehension. He generally takes his victims to a place where he controls the action, his "comfort zone" (Holmes & Holmes, 1994; Ressler & Shachtman, 1992, p. 120).

Less to control his victims than to instill terror in them, the sadistic rapist uses gags, duct tape, handcuffs, and other paraphernalia in the commission of his crimes. He may also blindfold his victims, also primarily to increase their fear. He may tell his victims what he plans to do to them, detail by detail, using excessive profanity and degrading language. As he is attacking his victim, he may call her by another name, perhaps his wife's or his mother's.

The sadistic rapist is very ritualistic. Each rape must go according to plan in order for him to experience the feelings he believes are necessary. He may need for his victims to say certain words to him for him to become aroused. Also, he may insist on oral sex as a prelude to coitus. Like the power assertive rapist, the sadistic rapist may suffer from retarded ejaculation. This rapist often carries in his vehicle a "rape kit" (Ressler & Shachtman, 1992); Ted Bundy, for example, carried a kit that included handcuffs, an ice pick, a ski mask, a mask made of panty hose, rope, black garbage bags, and a tire iron (see Figure 8.1).

As he continues his crimes, the sadistic rapist learns increasingly effective methods to stalk his victims and better ways of disposing of the bodies of those he has killed. For this rapist, murder is secondary. As Ted Bundy remarked to the first author during a 1985 interview while he was on death row at Florida State Prison, "A large number of serial killings [are] simply an attempt to silence the victims, a simple but effective means of elimination."

The sadistic rapist is often mildly intoxicated and may be a recreational drug user. He feels no remorse for his crimes, and will continue to rape until he is caught. It is not unusual for this offender

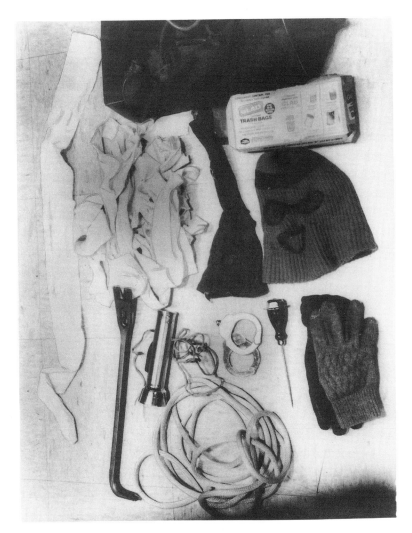

Figure 8.1. Ted Bundy: A Sadistic Rapist's Rape Kit

to escalate his violence to the point where the serial rapist becomes a serial killer.

Interviewing strategy. Unfortunately, there appears to be no one interviewing strategy that is generally effective with this type of rapist. As the Behavioral Science Unit of the FBI notes, this type of offender requires eclectic interviewing techniques. The interviewer must be aware of the many variables and nuances of the particular case, as this offender is highly unlikely to cooperate if he believes that the interviewer is anything less than competent and professional. Any interview of the sadistic rapist should be conducted in a businesslike manner, and the interviewer should be sure of the factual details of the case before presenting them to the offender.

Some researchers have suggested strategies for police interviews with suspected rapists in general. Hertica (1991, p. 39) proposes that a suspect be invited to come to the police station for the purpose of clarifying certain aspects of the case. In such a situation, the rapist may be anxious to give his side of the story. Hertica also notes that it is useful for the interviewing officer to try to build a rapport with the suspect; this may be aided by the interviewer's demonstrating some form of empathy with the suspect. As we have noted above, however, rapists are not all alike; it may be that these interviewing techniques will work with some but be detrimental with others.

CONCLUSION

Many people view rape as one of the most despicable crimes that may be committed against a human being. The by-products of rape can include the destruction of the victim's feelings of worth and the victim's internalization of feelings of responsibility for her own victimization. Although recent research on rape has tended to emphasize date or acquaintance rape over stranger rape, and the reported incidence of acquaintance rape has been increasing, the fact is that stranger rape still takes place. We believe that it is important to emphasize this point, in part because many of the kinds of rapists described in this chapter continue to escalate their acts of rape and may move to murder. The investigation and resolution of cases of stranger rape, in which sex is the weapon used in crimes of personal violence, require the concentrated efforts of law enforcement.

9. Pedophilia and Psychological Profiling

The sexual abuse of children is widely considered to be a heinous act. Most adults find both the etiology and the practice of child sexual abuse extremely difficult to understand, and so they tend to view those who prey on children as being simply "perverted" or mentally ill. After all, what mentally healthy person would rape a child? Further, it has been speculated in recent years that child sexual abuse is more common than was once thought. Even more disturbing is the assertion that child sex is increasingly tolerated in American society (Leo, 1993).

Unfortunately, there are adults who regard children as sex objects and as somehow deserving of exploitation as objects. For the person with such a mind-set, there is nothing wrong with sexually assaulting children. In fact, many child abusers apparently believe that children pursue adults for sex—an interesting rationalization that negates the adult's personal responsibility. From this perspective, the child is the cause, the prime mover; the molester is the victim.

DEFINITION OF TERMS

There are several levels of definitions of the terms *pedophile* and *child molester* (we use the two terms interchangeably here). One simple definition holds that a child molester is a person of majority age who engages in any type of sexual activity with individuals legally defined as children (minors). We believe that a more accurate and thus more useful definition would include such details about the molesters as their typical ages, the sexes of their victims, and their particular sexual behaviors. The above definition is devoid of the information needed to make it useful for those who want to understand the dynamics of the child offender or the behaviors the offender manifests, but it is at least a starting point. Those who must investigate cases involving child molesters or pedophiles, however, need a more complete definition. We take issue with the statement that "for law enforcement purposes, a child molester is simply an individual who engages in illegal sexual activity with children" (Leo, 1993, p. 37). This definition is too broad to have any usefulness for anyone interested in the criminal psychological assessment of child molesters.

The literal meaning of the word *pedophile* is "lover of children," and the phenomenon of pedophilia is just that simple, and that complex. The pedophile has a sexual interest in children that is manifested in victimization that can range from fondling to mutilation and murder. Not all pedophiles wish to harm children; some wish only to hold and fondle children, to show them "love." At the other extreme are sadistic pedophiles who achieve sexual gratification only with the death of a captive child.

Pedophiles' attraction to children, wide range of behaviors, and diversity of behaviors combine to make rehabilitation of these offenders extremely difficult, if not impossible. This is a topic that is beyond the scope of this book, however; our aim in this chapter, as in the rest of this volume, is to provide information useful to those who must investigate crimes.

The first step in investigating the crime of child molestation is to accept the definition of pedophilia as a perverse love of children, or, as the *Diagnostic and Statistical Manual of Mental Disorders* of the American Psychiatric Association (1994) defines it, "the acts or fantasy of engaging in sexual activity with prepubertal children as a repeatedly preferred or exclusive method of achieving sexual excitement." This is a classic definition that specifies the action involved (sexual), the age of the child victim (prepubertal), and the duration of the disorder (repeatedly or exclusive). A subtype of pedophile, the *hebephile* (a seldom-used term), prefers children who have reached puberty. This preference may be indicative of a type of child offender who makes distinctions in victim selection based solely on age. This may seem to be a minor point, but in the investigation of a case, the smallest detail can turn out to be pivotal for a successful resolution.

An added dimension in the investigation of child molestation cases, and one that is often confusing to law enforcement personnel, is the sex of the offender and the sex of the child victim as far as the issue of homosexuality/heterosexuality is concerned. Consider the following scenario. The police go to a home to arrest a man whom they are convinced must be a homosexual because he is suspected of molesting several young boys, but when they arrive at the man's home, they discover that he is married and has several children. This molester likely self-defines as heterosexual; he would never consider himself to be homosexual and would view having sex with an adult male as repugnant. Another possibility is that he is gay or bisexual and is in a heterosexual marriage for any of a variety of reasons. The point is that the presence of young male victims does not automatically mean that the offender is a gay male. Consider the case of John Gacy, who sexually molested and killed 33 young males in Chicago (he has been executed for his crimes). Gacy did not consider himself to be gay, and he was rankled when this was suggested to him (author's files). He may have been more accepting of the term *bisexual.* At any rate, the investigation of the Gacy case would have been severely impeded if it had focused solely on gay suspects.

Before we move on to present a typology of pedophiles, most of whom are male, we should note that women have also been known to be child molesters. However, when women commit this offense, it tends to receive meager attention in the media and from the courts. Women who victimize children also tend to attract less rage from the parents of their victims than do men who commit such crimes, especially when the child involved is an adolescent male. Some may even condone an adult woman's sexual contact with an adolescent boy as a "rite of passage" for the boy.

The majority of Americans find the sexual victimization of children abhorrent, and vast resources have been expended on the investigation of individuals as well as organizations that are intent on such victimization. Child molesters, like rapists and serial killers, differ from one another in motivations, activities, and so on, and information about these differences is invaluable for the development of profiles aimed at the apprehension of these offenders.

TYPOLOGY OF PEDOPHILES

As we have noted, all pedophiles are not the same. Just as the members of any group are in some ways different from one another, pedophiles are different in their behavioral patterns, selection of victims, use of lures, and propensity toward violence. Burgess, Groth, and Holmstrom (1978) categorize child abusers as "situational" or "preferential," and within their typology they include subtypes with distinguishing traits.

THE SITUATIONAL CHILD MOLESTER

The situational pedophile typically has fewer victims than the preferential child molester. This child molester does not have a true sexual interest in children, but will experiment with children when stress is introduced into his life. Also, this type of molester may sexually abuse not only children, but any vulnerable persons, such as the elderly or the physically or mentally impaired. Within the category of situational pedophiles there are several subtypes, which

Burgess et al. (1978) label regressed, morally indiscriminate, sexually indiscriminate, and naive or inadequate.

The *regressed pedophile* turns to children as objects for sexual gratification on a temporary basis as a result of some situational occurrence in his life that challenges his self-image and results in poor self-esteem. This type of molester may collect child pornography, but is not as likely to do so as is the fixated pedophile (described below). The regressed pedophile is generally involved with adults in normal relationships. He may have some interpersonal problems, but to all outward appearances he has no great problems in relating to adults in personal as well as sexual relationships. Psychologically, when under some type of situational stress, such as the breakup of a marriage or a negative experience in the workplace, this type of child offender experiences the child as a pseudoadult (Burgess et al., 1978). Often, this type of child molester is married and lives with his family. An illustration of the type of circumstances that might cause this kind of molester to victimize children is provided by the following, which was related to the first author in an interview:

I had never thought of molesting children. I was a deacon in my church, a Cub Scout leader, and a youth minister. I had been around children all my life with no intent to harm them. One day, I came home from work and my wife said that there was something she wanted to talk to me about. She said, "Tony, you physically disgust me and I never want you to touch me again!" This really affected me, as you can imagine. In the next 2 weeks, I was coming up for a big promotion, and I knew that if I did not get it I would never be promoted before I retired. I'm 60 years old and this would have been my last shot. It came down to me and a young fellow at work who was only 30 years old. He got the job.

I was crushed. That weekend, I and the Cub Scout troop went on a camping trip. As usual, there were two people to a pup tent, and there was a 9-year-old sharing a tent with me. It started raining and thundering and the boy got scared. He asked if he could come over to my side of the tent and climb into my sleeping bag. Well, one thing led to another and before long, I was fondling him. This led to other young boys, which went on for over a year.

This abuser was discovered when one of the molested children told some other children and finally the minister of his church what had happened to him. The molester was arrested, convicted, and sent to prison.

The regressed type of molester is generally apt to sexually abuse children he does not know, and the children are typically victims of opportunity (Holmes, 1991). His victims are most likely to be female; the abuser who related the preceding story molested young boys simply because they were available. The regressed child molester is generally geographically stable, employed, and married. He may have some problems with alcohol abuse and probably has low self-esteem.

The *morally indiscriminate* molester is an abuser of all available persons. For this offender, children are just another category of victims; he does not tend to have a particular preference for children as sexual partners. The *sexually indiscriminate* offender has a basic motivation toward sexual experimentation. He may be described as a "try-sexual"—that is, he is willing to try anything of a sexual nature. He may be involved in a wide variety of sexual practices, including tyndarianism (mate swapping), bondage and discipline, triolism, and other unusual practices. He may involve his biological children and/or his stepchildren in these sexual practices. This molester also has no particular sexual preference for children; they are simply there.

The final type of situational pedophile is the *naive* or *inadequate* child molester. This offender suffers from some form of mental disorder (e.g., retardation or senility) that renders him unable to make the distinction between right and wrong concerning sexual practices with children. Often, this type of molester's neighbors are aware of him; he may have a reputation in the community as being "strange" or "bizarre." He is a loner, usually not by choice but because he is not capable of establishing personal relationships with others. This type of predator usually does not physically harm children (Haas & Haas, 1990); he is most likely to experiment with children with sexual practices such as holding, fondling, kissing, and licking, but does not engage in sexual intercourse or oral or anal sex.

TABLE 9.1 Situational Child Molesters

	Regressed	Morally Indiscriminate	Sexually Indiscriminate	Inadequate
Basic traits	poor coping skills	user of people	sexual experimentation	social misfit
Motivation	substitution	why not?	boredom	insecurity and curiosity
Victim criteria	availability	vulnerability, opportunity	new and different	nonthreatening
Method of operation	coercion	lure, force, or manipulation	involve in existing activity	exploitation of size advantage
Porn collection	possible	S&M, detective magazines	highly likely	likely

SOURCE: Adapted from National Center for Missing and Exploited Children (1985, p. 8).

Children are nonthreatening, and so the molester feels more in control of this form of relationship than in ones that involve adults. If this offender has a collection of pornography, it is typically not of the child porn genre.

Table 9.1 lists the characteristics typical of the various types of situational child molesters.

THE PREFERENTIAL CHILD MOLESTER

Situational child molesters, especially the morally and sexually indiscriminate types, are the perpetrators of many cases of severe child sexual abuse. However, the large number of pedophiles who can be classified as preferential child molesters are more likely to be very dangerous to children. These molesters look at children as providers of pleasure; as the label attached to this type of pedophile suggests, the persons in this group of abusers *prefer* children over adults as providers of sexual gratification. Within the broad category of preferential molesters there are several subtypes, including the sadistic pedophile, the seductive molester, and the fixated molester.

The *sadistic pedophile,* or *mysoped* (Holmes, 1991), has made a vital connection between sexual gratification and fatal violence. This kind of child molester's assault invariably ends with the death of the child. Typically, this aggressive offender chooses child victims who are strangers to him. It appears also that he may stalk his victims rather than use any form of seduction (the method typical of many pedophiles). The mysoped will often abduct a child from places where children gather: playgrounds, schools, shopping centers, and so on. He will usually not attempt to induce the child to go with him; he simply takes the child by force. The abduction is followed by a scenario that includes pain inflicted upon the child, followed by the child's death.

This type of pedophile has no "love" of children in the traditional sense. He is interested only in causing harm and death to a vulnerable victim over whom he feels great superiority. The mysoped inflicts fatal physical harm on the victim and then often mutilates the victim's body. If the victim is a young boy, the child's penis may be cut off and inserted into the child's mouth. Small girls are also brutally assaulted, with the physical violence often directed toward the child's genitals. This sexual sadist often terrorizes the child with some type of weapon; the crime is premeditated and ritualized.

There have been many well-known cases involving mysopeds. One example is the case of Westley Dodd, who was executed for his crimes in the state of Washington. Dodd was an aggressive and sadistic child offender. He was considered a loner in high school, where he was a member of the high school band. Many of his high school teachers thought he was honest and dependable; his band teacher, for example, remarked that Dodd was quiet, always did what he was told, and was not a behavioral problem. In an interview with Dr. Al Carlisle, a psychologist from Utah, Dodd stated that he considered himself a humanitarian sociopath. He said that if a child fell off his bicycle, he would be the first to reach the child and tender aid. How, he asked Carlisle, could he intend to do so much pain and suffering to children whom he also loved in the way that he did?

Dodd killed three young boys, two brothers and another 5-year-old child. Dodd abducted his last victim, Lee Isely, from a public park while the boy's slightly older brother played nearby with some friends. Dodd took the boy home with him and over a period of several hours sexually abused him, which resulted in the child's death. Dodd then placed the body in a closet and went to work; when he returned later in the afternoon, he retrieved and committed anal sex and other forms of sexual abuse on the boy's body before disposing of the corpse. Dodd was apprehended by police as he attempted to abduct a fourth young boy at a neighborhood theater.

Albert Fish, known as the "moon maniac," was a sadistic child offender who was active in the early part of the twentieth century. Fish, an elderly, grandfatherly type, was finally arrested in New York after years of careful investigation. When he was arrested, police found in his home body parts that apparently came from various children. His final victim, Grace Budd, was taken from the Budd home by Fish under the pretense that he was taking her to attend a birthday party on Long Island. He transported the girl to an abandoned area, killed her, and then cooked portions of her body for his own consumption. More than a pedophile and a cannibal, Fish was also involved in infibulation, or self-torture of one's own sexual body parts. After his execution in the electric chair at Sing Sing, an autopsy revealed that he had 29 sewing needles implanted in his penis and scrotum (Schechter, 1990).

The *seductive molester* entices children by "courting them" with attention, affection, and gifts. This kind of molester may court a child over an extended period of time and may be involved with several children at the same time. This molester is similar to the *fixated molester,* who desires affection from children, or, as Johnston, French, Schouweiler, and Johnston (1992) put it, has "a cynical need for affection" (p. 620). This kind of child offender is not really developed past the point where he, as a child, found other children attractive and desirable. In other words, he has become "fixed" at an early stage of psychosexual development (Burgess et al., 1978). The fixated type of child molester's interest in children as sexual partners starts in adolescence. Unlike the regressed child offender, this offender requires no precipitating cause before he turns to child sexual abuse; his interest in children is persistent and compulsive. The fixated offender generally prefers male victims.

The fixated child offender generally has little or no activity with age-mates, usually is single, and is considered to be immature and uncomfortable around other adults. He is often childlike in his lifestyle and behaviors. According to Burg (1983), many pedophiles of this type select children as sexual objects because children are less demanding, more easily dominated, and less critical of their partners' performance than are adults.

The fixated child offender is not interested in physically harming the child. He loves children and does not desire to do anything that might harm them. He courts a child, buys the child gifts as a seduction ploy, and slowly becomes intimate with the child. Oral-genital sex is the norm, and actual intercourse develops only after a generous period of time has passed (Holmes, 1991, p. 38).

PROFILING CHILD MOLESTERS

It is important to remember that the various types of child molesters differ in their victimization rituals, methods of victim selection, and abduction processes (Knight, Carter, & Prentky, 1989; Okami & Goldberg, 1992). We have decided to limit our examination of the traits common to various child molester types to those offenders who are likely to molest children most often and who are likely to come into contact with the criminal justice system. We discuss below the immature offender, the regressed offender, the sadistic offender, and the fixated offender.

Table 9.2 lists selected characteristics of these four kinds of offenders that are important in the profiling process. The alert investigator will consider these characteristics when examining cases involving children, such as cases of abduction, molestation, and even murder.

Concerning the first listed trait in the table, "harmful to the child," we should note that we are referring only to physical harm. It is unclear exactly what mental and psychological damage is done to a child when he or she is used by an adult for sexual pleasure, and we do not attempt to measure that here. (Some research has indicated that children who are sexually victimized by adults tend to abuse children themselves when they reach adulthood [see Holmes, 1973];

TABLE 9.2 Profiling: Child Molesters

Element	Immature Offender	Regressed Offender	Sadistic Offender	Fixated Offender
Harmful to the child	no	no	yes	no
Aggressive personality	no	no	yes	no
Antisocial personality	no	no	yes	no
Child sexual preference	no	yes	yes	yes
Child a stranger	no	no	yes	no
Intercourse occurs	no	yes	yes	no
Neighborhood stalk	yes	no	no	no
Abduction of the child	no	no	yes	no
Computer bulletin board user	no	no	yes	yes
Large number of child victims	no	no	yes	yes
Intends fatal violence	no	no	yes	no
Uses seduction	no	yes	no	yes

this possibility has important implications for the investigatory process.) Of the types of child molesters discussed here, only the sadistic offender is purposely intent on inflicting physical harm on the child victim, and this invariably results in the death of the child.

As noted above, the sadistic offender has an aggressive and antisocial personality. He is best described as a sociopath. He may have a criminal record, because his sociopathy and aggressive personality may lead him to be involved in a variety of violent crimes, such as rape and assault.

The immature or naive offender does not generally prefer a particular sex of child victim (Harris, 1994), in contrast with the regressed offender, who tends to prefer female victims (although, as in the case of the Cub Scout leader described above, there are exceptions that are influenced by victim availability), and the sadistic offender, who prefers young boys. The sadistic molester often will mutilate his young victims, even to the extent of decapitation; he may also cut off the penis and insert it into the victim's mouth or anus. This is not to say that this offender will not victimize girls, but he more often assaults boys.

The fixated offender prefers young boys as sexual targets. As we have noted, the fixated pedophile likely selects children as sexual objects because they are less demanding, more easily dominated, and less critical of their partners' performance than are adults (Burg, 1983). As we have already seen, the label of *fixated* is applied to this offender because he is fixed at a certain point in his psychosexual development; the fact that the preferred targets are young boys may be seen as an indication of the offender's homosexuality. It is very unusual for a fixated offender to victimize young girls, although it is not unheard of. It is possible that a large proportion of active pedophiles may be classified as fixated pedophiles; if this is true, it has major implications for estimates of the proportion of all pedophiles who are homosexual versus heterosexual. Many researchers believe that the percentage of pedophiles who are homosexual is quite low; Freund and Watson (1992), for instance, estimate that the ratio of heterosexual pedophiles to homosexual pedophiles is 11:1. This is an area that will certainly benefit from further research.

The sadistic offender is the only one of the types of offenders discussed who will attack a child who is a complete stranger to him. This offender is apt to conduct a sudden or blitz attack on a child after only a minor stalk. He uses no seduction process, only a quick abduction and then the complete victimization of the child, ending with the murder.

The sex acts perpetrated against a child also vary from one type of molester to another. For example, with the immature offender, the molestation might take the form of holding, fondling, kissing; with the regressed offender, the desired act may be anal sodomy (with male victims) or vaginal penetration (with girls) as well as oral sodomy. The sadistic offender's attack will include sex that is intended to harm the victim physically, including the removal of body parts, often while the victim is still alive. This offender uses anal sex because of the physical pain it causes the victim. The fixated offender, in contrast, will perform oral sex upon the victim, but there is a sense of positive affect directed toward the victim.

Immature and regressed offenders are more apt to be geographically stable than are sadistic and fixated types, for obvious reasons. The fixated offender, in contrast, may move from one area of the country to another in his search for victims, taking some time in each area to find and cultivate children to victimize. This molester is apt to move into an area, victimize children, and then move on to another area. He may leave of his own accord, or, if he has been apprehended, he may be given a choice as to whether to stay and face prosecution or move on to another area. In one community, for example, when a molester of more than 100 young boys was arrested, the judge offered him the choice of returning to his home country of England or staying in the community and being prosecuted. The offender, of course, chose the former. In effect, he became another community's problem.

The sadistic child molester is also likely to be geographically transient. He may be employed for brief periods, but he is not likely to form long-lasting personal relationships; he usually moves on very quickly after a fatal victimization.

As the age of technology advances even into the world of child sexual victimization, computers are being used by some sadistic and fixated types of child molesters as they search for victims. Some computer bulletin boards advertise sexual proposals that may also include veiled ads for children. Knowledge about this development can be useful to law enforcement personnel who are investigating child abuse cases. For example, Detective Walt Parsons of the Arvada (Colorado) Police Department (personal communication, 1995) has reported some success in using computer bulletin boards in his investigations of such cases.

The profiling process can be useful in the investigation of child molestation if the investigator is cognizant of the extent of victimization committed by the offender, the behavior of the offender, and other behavioral and social patterns. For example, if the child victim in a case has been killed, it may be that the offender is a mysoped, especially if there has been mutilation of the body or there is any evidence of anal sodomy or other gross physical injuries. If a child victim reports that an older male was the perpetrator of a molestation, the alert investigator will ask the child about the nature of the acts committed. If they include such things as licking, kissing, and fondling but no more overt sexual acts, this is indicative of an offender of the regressed or immature type. An additional element the profiler should consider is whether or not the offender is a stranger to his victims. If the offender is a complete stranger, this would tend to eliminate the immature molester, as this abuser generally lives within the neighborhood and knows the children, who are sometimes even the offender's own relatives (Margolin, 1994).

The preferential child molester, especially the fixated or sadistic pedophile, is more likely than the situational offender to have a collection of child pornography. The victimization of children, even to the extreme of homicide, is in a way a "style of life" for the preferential molester. Thus, it is likely that such pornography will play an integral part in the fantasy life of this molester. The character of the pornography preferred by this type of offender tends to be that depicting violent sex acts. One pedophile interviewed by the first author stated that the pornography he desired came mostly from detective story magazines and spoke of violence directed toward children. The alert investigator should include such material in any application for a search warrant.

The number of children any given molester will abuse varies. There may be a few child molesters in prison who have abused only one child, but they are undoubtedly the exception rather than the rule. Some believe that many pedophiles abuse hundreds of children (Briere & Runtz, 1989; Holmes, 1991, p. 31). Furthermore, as we have mentioned previously, the outlook for the rehabilitation of child molesters is not considered hopeful (see, e.g., Connors, 1992; Freeman-Longo & Wall, 1986; Proulx, Cote, & Achille, 1993).

CONCLUSION

Clearly, the sexual abuse of children cannot be tolerated. It is an important responsibility of the criminal justice enterprise to detect and apprehend those who perpetrate violence against our most treasured, and vulnerable, asset. The profiling process can be a useful tool in the investigation and apprehension of those who victimize children. Future researchers should make a concentrated effort to identify further the social and demographic characteristics of child molesters, as well as their typical behavioral and criminal activities (Abel, Lawry, Karstrom, Osborn, & Gillespie, 1994). With such information, profilers can better aid in stopping such offenders, be they the very violent or those who have no intent of physically harming children but do immeasurable psychological damage.

10. Geography, Profiling, and Predatory Criminals

Psychological profiling has been used as an investigative tool for a relatively short period of time. Although it is true that profiling has not been universally accepted by the law enforcement community, the procedure is becoming increasingly accepted by police officers. It is still vital to practice the time-proven methods of successful investigation: careful preservation of the crime scene, meticulous collection of physical evidence, thorough interviewing of all witnesses, and so on. However, the investigator must also be aware of the latest scientific techniques, such as DNA testing and linguistic profiling, to maximize the chances of successful case resolution. One relatively recent development within the profiling field is the analysis of suspects' geographic patterns in an effort to determine where their residences are located.

The role that geography plays in the criminal profiling process is still unclear, but it is an issue deserving of further research and study. Up to now, the importance of geography has not been stressed, but

AUTHORS' NOTE: This chapter was written by Ronald M. Holmes and D. Kim Rossmo.

there are many indications that the analysis of criminal mobility and an understanding of the geographic characteristics of crime scenes hold significant promise for the advancement of investigative profiling.

DISTANCE

Perceptions of distances vary from person to person, and sometimes tend to vary from region to region. We have sometimes been surprised, for instance, at the differing attitudes about distances that seem to be displayed by people who live in various parts of the United States. For instance, a colleague from Utah, Dr. Al Carlisle, thinks little of driving several hundred miles, interviewing someone, and then driving home the same day. For an individual in another part of the country (or, for that matter, a different person in Utah), a trip of 100 miles might be considered an occasion demanding an overnight stay in the city of destination before the return trip the next day. Perceptions of distance are relative, and they depend upon a variety of different elements (Douglas, Burgess, Burgess, & Ressler, 1992). Stea (1969) lists some of the influences on the perception of distance as follows:

- Method of transportation
- Attractiveness of origins, destinations, and travel ways
- Familiarity of roads and highways
- Number and types of barriers
- Alternative routes
- Actual distance

For the purposes of profiling in crime investigation, both perceived distance and actual distance are important elements.

METHOD OF TRANSPORTATION

The perception of distance is naturally influenced by the mode of transportation. For example, a distance one must walk seems much greater than that same distance traveled in a car. Obviously, a killer who must walk to a crime scene, or who must depend upon public transportation, will clearly have a more constricted range of activities than will a killer who has a vehicle at his disposal.

One murderer whose case we profiled traveled by city bus because he had neither a driver's license nor an automobile. He killed and assaulted within the immediate area of his home, and his range of travel was restricted to within his own neighborhood. The hunting area was immediate to his personal activities and was determined not only by his daily actions, but also by his personality. He was a disorganized personality who saw visions and heard voices. His restricted comfort zone was defined by his daily activities, limited by the range and mode of his travels and by his own personal inadequacies.

ATTRACTIVENESS OF ORIGINS, DESTINATIONS, AND TRAVEL WAYS

We all have certain roads and highways that we prefer to travel, for reasons that vary from person to person. It may be that there are fewer regulated stops along one route than along another. It may be that a road is particularly attractive. There is an expressway in Kentucky, for example, that wanders through the thoroughbred horse farms. There is also a highway connecting the same cities that cuts through a strip-mining area characterized by huge, gaping holes in the earth. Obviously, based on the criterion of visual attractiveness, the former is the preferable route for most people. However, other factors also enter into individuals' decisions as to which routes to take, such as their travel origination and destination points. The point of origin and the point of destination exert, respectively, "push" and "pull" factors on the individual. The exact nature and character of such forces in a given criminal case are known only to the individual offender, but the alert investigator will be able, at least to some extent, to get into the mind of the criminal and make some reasonable assumptions (as protagonist Will Graham does in the novel *The Red Dragon*; see Chapter 2).

FAMILIARITY OF ROADS AND HIGHWAYS

Human beings are all, to one degree or another, creatures of habit. We repeat those things that are familiar and comfortable to us. For example, some families take their vacations in the same places year after year. There are obvious reasons for this: Familiarity brings comfort; the routes of travel become memorized, and road maps are no longer needed; landmarks are easily recognized and anticipated as a means of validating that the correct route is being traveled.

As one gets to know an area's roads and highways, along with topographic elements and landmarks, familiarity leads to comfort and reassurance, and this affects the subjective perception of distance. Such elements can have an impact on where an offender cruises for victims or searches for places to dispose bodies. The more familiar the offender is with a highway or road, the more locations he will be aware of that will serve his criminal purposes.

NUMBER AND TYPES OF BARRIERS

Geographic barriers and boundaries, such as rivers, freeways, railroad tracks, jurisdictional and state lines, and national borders, also affect individuals' choices of routes and methods of travel. An offender facing a decision such as whether or not to cross a river in the hunt for victims must weigh certain factors. How much of a barrier is the river? What is the distance to the nearest bridge? Is he comfortable enough, psychologically, to operate on the other side of the river? Is there a county or state line involved, and, if so, what are the advantages and disadvantages and the various legal issues surrounding crossing that boundary? The investigator must take into account such considerations when examining the geographic landscape surrounding a crime scene.

ALTERNATIVE ROUTES

If there are only a few major roads in a community, an offender will quickly become aware not only of the avenues of travel but also of the possibilities for criminal behavior held by each. When several arterial routes exist in a community, however, there are additional elements to consider. Which road is the most direct? Which is the most pleasant to travel? Which has the lowest risk of detection? These are all important considerations. The existence of multiple possible routes will enhance the capability of the offender to find, and flee, desirable locations.

ACTUAL DISTANCE

The actual distance between two points has obvious implications for the travel of an offender. No matter what the perceived distance is, actual distance necessarily affects the time it takes to travel between the points; also, choices among alternative routes may be influenced by the actual distances they require the individual to travel.

MENTAL MAPS

We all have mental maps, or cognitive images of our spatial surroundings that have been built up over time during daily activities and experiences. Most of these maps are of the areas around our homes, workplaces, recreation sites, favorite shopping districts, and the like—neighborhoods that are known to us and familiar. Connecting the centers of activity in our mental maps are various routes, such as paths, streets, bridges, and highways; separating them are various physical and psychological barriers, such as buildings, rivers, ravines, brush, and lakes. Based on the information in his or her mental maps, a person chooses the paths to use during daily routine travels. A mental map, like a traditional map of a geographic area, provides a spatial image from which a person can get his or her bearings. Lynch (1960) lists some of the elements that make up a spatial image:

- *Paths:* routes of travel (e.g., streets, railroad tracks, paths)

- *Edges:* borders or lines (e.g., river edge, lakeshore, city limits)
- *Districts:* distinct and identifiable areas (e.g., financial district, Chinatown, Skid Row)
- *Nodes:* focused centers of activity (e.g., intersections, subway stations, plazas)
- *Landmarks:* geographic reference points (e.g., mountains, towers, billboards)

Because mental maps are affected by activity sites, we should remember that, for the experienced criminal, such locations may include courthouses, prisons and jails, criminal justice agencies, areas of prostitution, previous crime sites, and so on. It may be that we should return to an examination of the "concentric zone theory" of years past to develop a theory of the relationship between criminal profiling and geography; but perhaps it is just as effective to consider our thoughts regarding our own mental maps and spatial behavior.

CRIMINALS AND MOBILITY

One of the main items of interest to us in the examination of the Ted Bundy case, in addition to the number of victims he admitted having killed over a 17-year murder career (first author's files), was the manner in which he drove the highways of our nation. Holmes and De Burger (1988) term Bundy a geographically transient serial murderer, meaning that he killed first in one area and then moved to another area and killed again. In an interview with the first author, Bundy stated that "this person we are talking about," Bundy himself, may have killed in as many as nine states. Only the night before his death did he admit to a murder in a tenth state, Idaho.

The U.S. highway system makes it possible for a predator to travel long distances, not only in search of potential victims, but also in an effort to confuse law enforcement. Additionally, extensive road networks provide vast numbers of opportunities for the disposal of bodies. For example, in the case of the Hillside Stranglers in California (O'Brien, 1985), most of the victims' bodies were dumped close to the freeway, and the killers were able to be back on the road within seconds.

In investigating a murder, it is important to ask why the killer decided to search that particular neighborhood for a victim, why he chose a particular area to dump the body, and why he picked the particular travel route he did. What were the geographic characteristics that made the victim selection area, body disposal location, and route of travel so attractive? These choices on the part of the offender should not be considered to be mere accident.

Consider the following case. A serial rapist admitted, after his arrest, to more than 30 rapes. The attacks commenced when his wife refused to engage is sexual relations because she was fearful of pregnancy. Her refusal, he later admitted, launched him into a mental state in which he both feared and hated women. To ventilate his hatred and help control his fear, he repeatedly raped, but with little overt violence. (From the model of personal violence discussed in Chapter 6, we can see that he progressed from the distorted thinking stage to the fall.) This offender's rapes took on an interesting geographic pattern. The first rape occurred on the direct route from his home to his work; it was less than a block from his commuting path to the apartment of the victim. The next few victims were attacked further away, but all off of his main route. The rapist later admitted to police that he often left home early to search for suitable victims along the route he traveled to work. Eventually, the rapist moved to a new address; he began to explore other directions looking for victims, but again, never traveled more than a block from the main thoroughfare. This rapist is best categorized as a power reassurance rapist with many of the characteristics of the disorganized (asocial) personality type (Knight & Prentky, 1987). He felt most comfortable in his travels along routes that were familiar and where he felt personally secure.

In evaluating more than 800 murder cases, we have made some interesting discoveries regarding the distances traveled by offenders in the commission of their crimes. We have plotted the travel of serial offenders—rapists, murderers, and child abusers—and it is clear that offender mobility and crime site geography are not only important, but predictable. As the neophyte criminal progresses in the "industry of offending," he gains experience that leads to increases in his comfort and confidence levels. With this increasing sense of comfort and confidence comes an expansion in predatory spatial activity—the offender's travel distances and victim search areas increase in size. When a serial offender starts to hunt, the first few acts are usually situated relatively close to the location of either his home or his work site. As initial successes lead to increased confidence, the offender becomes willing to seek his prey further and further from home.

If an investigator is convinced that certain crimes have been committed by a serial offender, he or she should give special consideration to the locations connected to the first few crimes. If it appears that a single person is responsible for multiple crimes, and if the site pattern is spreading, then it may be that the locations of the earliest crimes are close to the home or workplace of the offender, in his "comfort zone."

GEOGRAPHY AND VICTIM SELECTION

Crimes suitable for geographic analysis are those in which the offender exercises some spatial decision-making process. The most obvious of these are crimes of a predatory nature, in which the criminal hunts for victims, choosing the neighborhoods in which he plans to seek out suitable targets. Not only must the perpetrator pick the areas in which he will look for victims, but he must also determine where he will dump or bury their bodies, what routes he will travel, and the mode of transportation he will use. The degree of offender movement or travel varies depending on the type and characteristics of the perpetrator (Hickey, 1991). Serial crimes are the easiest to develop geographic profiles for, as each different crime site contains new spatial information, providing the profiler with multiple sources of data. Serial murder, serial rape, and serial arson are the most common offenses profiled in this manner, but the principles can be applied to a variety of other crimes.

Rossmo (1994, 1995, in press) describes a series of geographic zones, derived from Brantingham and Brantingham's (1981) model

Home   **Work**

Shopping and Entertainment

Figure 10.1. Offender Activity Space

of target selection, within which an offender is most likely to commit crimes. The areas of "home," "work," and "shopping and entertainment" constitute comfort zones that allow predatory offenders to cruise and commit their crimes under a psychological blanket of protection (see Figure 10.1). Ted Bundy created cemeteries in such places as Taylor Mountain and Lake Sammanish State Park. His dump sites were close to the Washington State highway system, situated in areas with which he was familiar and in which he felt a sense of psychological comfort.

The predator has a zone of behavioral activity, a space that contains both activity sites and the connecting paths between those sites. The serial rapist whose case we mentioned previously in this chapter had activity sites situated within his home and work neighborhoods and shopping and entertainment areas. His connecting routes were the main streets that ran from one activity to another.

Rossmo (1994, 1995, in press) notes that geography plays an important role in the offender's selection of "suitable" victims. What defines a suitable victim? Why is it that some predators will let one potential victim pass and wait for another? It has to be more than the physical characteristics of the victim; there has to be a "click" within the mind of the predator that alerts him to a sense of "rightness" for attack. When a criminal selects a target, he must also have some kind of feeling about "the rightness of the place." Is the area appropriate for predation? Does it contain sufficient and suitable victims? Is it familiar? Does it give the offender a feeling of comfort? Is the risk of apprehension low? Are there escape routes? As the offender considers these factors, so must the profiler.

THE NATURE OF GEOGRAPHIC PROFILING

Geographic analysis is only one of several potential sources of information in the successful investigation of serial crimes. In the thorough investigation of any such case, all of the following play a part (Rossmo, 1995):

- Crime scene similarities
- Traditional investigative techniques
- Linkage analysis
- Psychological profiling
- Geographic profiling
- New investigative strategies

Some of these are well known to police and citizens alike. For example, we are all alert to the possibility of identifying the perpetrators of similar crimes by matching the MOs or signatures evident at the crime scenes.

When a series of crimes show similarities that suggest they were committed by the same offender, police agencies now have a variety of investigative options at their disposal. Traditional investigative techniques will always be the mainstay of detective work. In addition, linkage analysis can identify connections between similar crimes committed in different jurisdictions. Such analyses are usually performed at the state or national level through the use of computerized systems, such as the FBI's Violent Criminal Apprehension Program (VICAP), the Royal Canadian Mounted Police's Violent Crime Linkage Analysis System (VICLAS), the New York State Police's

Homicide Assessment and Lead Tracking Project (HALT), and the Washington State Attorney General's Office's Homicide Investigation Tracking System (HITS).

Not only can linkage analysis systems locate possible suspects from records of similar past offenses, but they also provide, through the identification of similar crimes, maximum information for psychological and geographic profiling efforts. The development of both psychological and geographic profiles, used in a complementary fashion, may lead to new investigative strategies that can be employed to help solve serial crimes.

CONSIDERATIONS IN GEOGRAPHIC PROFILING

There is no single method that will absolutely identify an unknown offender, and the investigator would be wise to consider the various methods available as complementary. This is especially true when one considers the impact of geography on criminal profiling. Some of the factors that are important to consider in the construction of a geographic profile are as follows (Rossmo, 1995):

- Crime location type
- Arterial roads and highways
- Physical and psychological boundaries
- Land use
- Neighborhood demographics
- Routine activities of victims
- Displacement

Each of these is addressed in turn below.

CRIME LOCATION TYPE

The designation of a site as a crime location depends on the particular offense and the perpetrator's modus operandi. Many violent crimes involve several different locations; for instance, Rossmo (in press) lists the following locations that might be connected to offenses of murder or rape:

- Encounter site
- Attack site
- Crime site
- Victim disposal site
- Vehicle dump site

The geographic pattern of the crime sites will also be influenced by the mode of travel available to the criminal. An offender who walks, for example, will have a more constricted hunting area than will an offender who has access to a vehicle.

The location where the offender first contacts the victim is termed the *encounter site*. This may be in a bar, on the street, in a park, in a red-light district, or any other location where the victim and the offender share physical and psychological space. The *attack site* is the location where the offender first attacks the victim. It is often the same as the encounter site. In such cases, it may be that the offender lives relatively close to this position. When there are two different locations for the encounter and the attack, this suggests that the personality of the offender may be more developed, indicating capability for growth in the range of travel in the search for victims. In other words, this type of offender is more likely to be of the organized personality type.

The *crime site* is the location of the actual crime—the murder or rape scene, for example. The *victim disposal site* is the location where the offender dumps or releases the victim. If the victim disposal site is different from the encounter, attack, and crime locations, then we would suspect that the offender has an organized personality; not only would he be capable of elaborate planning, but he would also be willing to travel long distances. If the locations are the same for all parts of the crime, then we have reason to believe that the offender is more likely to be disorganized, because this type of personality is most comfortable in familiar neighborhoods. Since the more organized offender usually travels longer distances to stalk, attack, or dispose of his victims, it is more likely that this type of offender lives further from the initial contact site (Barret, 1990). The same argument can be applied to the other types of crime locations. It should be stressed that often these different crime sites are in the same location. Every case has to be viewed separately, because each crime is unique, even if the offender and his signature are the same.

ARTERIAL ROADS AND HIGHWAYS

In any area, people have preferences for the roads that they travel. These preferred routes depend upon a variety of things. One road, for example, may have a more pleasant view than another; another may be especially suitable for travel on foot or by bicycle. For those traveling by car, the choice of which street to take may depend on the number of stop signs or stop lights they will encounter, or the directness of the route. It is safe to say that no one road, despite how planners have laid out the thoroughfare, will be the favorite route of everyone in the area.

Camelback Road, for example, is one of the main routes between Phoenix and Scottsdale, Arizona. Along this street are numerous businesses, new and used car dealers, restaurants, and stop lights. When we asked for directions from Phoenix to Scottsdale while in Arizona on a speaking engagement, we were told that the best way to get there was via another road, less traveled, less direct, but with little to detract the view of the driver and passenger, and with less pleasant topography. Which route is the better depends on one's needs—the quickest way or the most visually appealing. The choice will depend not only on the person but on the circumstances and purpose of the travel. Would a person travel one road to work and a different one to commit a crime? The answer may depend upon the personality type, circumstances, and purpose of the offender.

PHYSICAL AND PSYCHOLOGICAL BOUNDARIES

Physical and psychological barriers and boundaries also exist in our travels. Rivers and railroad tracks act as physical barriers; in some cases these barriers cannot be physically crossed, whereas in others they can if the traveler chooses to do so. Such choices on the part of offenders may not be initially comprehensible to investigators, but they make sense from the criminals' standpoint. Psychological barriers can come from the discomfort people often feel when they are in unfamiliar areas, such as neighborhoods of socioeconomic or racial composition different from their own. The hunting patterns of offenders may also be distorted by such influences.

LAND USE

The dominant land use in the areas surrounding, and between, crime sites is important in a geographic analysis. What is the zoning in those areas—residential, commercial, industrial, or parkland? Are there major attractions nearby, such as shopping centers, bars, entertainment sites, parks, office towers, or factories? Are there important transportation sites within those areas, such as train stations, bus routes, freeways, jogging paths, or subway stops? The way that the surrounding areas are utilized can provide vital information—in effect, geographic clues—that may significantly assist in the investigation of serial crimes.

NEIGHBORHOOD DEMOGRAPHICS

Related to land use information is demographic and census data. What are the characteristics of the populations that reside in the neighborhoods where the crime sites are located? Information on sex ratios, racial composition, age breakdowns, occupational groups, socioeconomic status, crime rates, and other demographic variables is important in any profiling process.

ROUTINE ACTIVITIES OF VICTIMS

The behavior, travels, and habits of the victims are critical elements in the profiling process and are especially important in any geographic analysis. Certain inferences can be drawn if the body dump site in a murder case is located in a place that would not be expected considering the victim's normal range of behaviors and interests. In such a case it may be assumed that the location of the dump site has more significance to the offender than to the victim. It is also important to consider the manner in which the body was dumped or displayed, as that may give some indication of the characteristics of the offender.

DISPLACEMENT

The spatial patterns of the crime locations may change as the offender progresses through his crime series, maturing and gaining confidence, and learning how to expand his hunting areas. Further, geographic displacement may occur because an offender has changed the locations of his criminal activities (e.g., victim hunting areas, body dump sites) in response to some action taken on the part of law enforcement agencies. Patrol saturation efforts by the police in targeted neighborhoods are the most common cause of displacement. Inappropriate media disclosures have also led organized offenders to change their MOs and often their geographic patterns. Profilers must be aware of, and take into consideration, the possible influences of such factors.

In summary, we suggest that profilers must be aware of the geography of the areas relevant to their investigations. They should plot the crime locations on a map and look for patterns. Are there industries, residential areas, or shopping and entertainment centers along the routes between the crime sites? This seemingly old-fashioned approach is a first step in the application of geographic analysis. The profiler must look for relationships among the offender's areas of activity.

COMPUTERIZED GEOGRAPHIC ANALYSES

At a recent national criminal justice conference, speakers discussed psychological profiling, geographic profiling, and other new scientific advances in this area. Among the advances discussed was a computer program, Criminal Geographic Targeting (CGT), that assesses the spatial characteristics of crimes. The program scans every known point in the offender's hunting area and then produces a topographic map, similar to a relief map of a mountain range, that assigns probabilities to different points for the location of the offender's residence. As Rossmo (1994) notes, this program is one useful strategy for information management in cases of serial crimes.

Most major crime cases that are serial in nature suffer from the problem of information overload. Often, thousands of tips will be received and hundreds of suspects developed, and this volume of data places tremendous demands on limited police resources. One of the major values of profiling is that it can provide a means for prioritizing leads and suspects. As many sources of information are address based, geographic profiling is particularly useful for strategic information management.

Because CGT produces a map that shows probable sites for offender residence by area, it can be employed as the basis for a variety of investigative strategies, the use of which depends upon the specific details of the case. Some of these strategies include the following:

- Patrol saturation and static stakeouts
- Door-to-door canvassing, grid, and area searches
- Suspect prioritization
- Computerized searches of police information and record systems
- Searches of outside agency databases
- Task force tip prioritization
- Zip/postal code prioritization

In one serial case, a child was abducted from near her home, murdered, and her body dumped in the outskirts of the city. Investigators had only a brief description of the suspect vehicle from a young playmate of the victim. A geographic profile was constructed using CGT, and the prioritized zip codes were used, in conjunction with the vehicle description, in an off-line database search of

Department of Motor Vehicles owner registration records. The end result was that thousands of potential suspect vehicles were narrowed down to only a few dozen, greatly facilitating the investigative process.

The typical construction of a geographic profile involves the following steps (Rossmo, 1994):

1. A thorough perusal of the case file, including investigation reports, witness statements, autopsy reports, and psychological profile (if available)
2. Detailed examination of crime scene and area photographs
3. Interviews with lead investigators and crime analysts
4. Visits, when possible, to each of the crime sites
5. Analysis of demographic data and neighborhood crime statistics
6. Study of street, land use, and transit maps
7. Computerized analysis (if appropriate)
8. Interim and final report writing

In this whole process, which takes on average about 2 weeks to complete, the computerized analysis involves less than 5% of the total time, and its use requires judicious decision making on the part of the profiler. Thus, although computers play an important role, their function should be placed in the proper perspective. We must always remember that profiling is still more of an art than a science, and it is only viable when the human element comes into play. A computer system, regardless of its sophistication, cannot include all the multitude of details involved in a given case, or comprehend the complete range of potential human behavior. The development of computerized profiling programs involving expert systems is an important advance, but the widespread availability of such technology is some years away. For now, we still need humans who are schooled in the disciplines of criminology, sociology, psychology, geography, and psychiatry—and a little luck.

CONCLUSION

The role of geography has been ignored too often in the profiling process. In this chapter we have examined some of the general principles of geographic profiling and crime scene assessment. Much of the material presented here is gleaned from the research and experiences of Rossmo and others who have worked in this area. Some of the insights we have offered we have gained through the process of profiling cases for police departments across the nation. By blending all this information, we have presented a plan that allows for a consideration of the role of geography and topography in the profiling process. We want to emphasize, however, that it is critical to retain the human factor in our understanding of the influence of geography. Then, and only then, can we be successful.

11. Computer Database Construction for Psychological Profiling

The ability to profile violent offenders successfully and consistently is in part a gift reserved to certain individuals who can reach inside the criminal mind and understand it. However, with certain information and the help of computer technology, all practitioners may be able to identify specific types of offenders. To do so, an investigator must have three things: access to all of the information on a case, general knowledge of similar cases/offenders nationwide, and, most important, knowledge of similar cases that have occurred.

This chapter is intended expressly for practitioners, so we assume that you have at your disposal all the facts of the cases with which you are concerned. Also, given the information provided in the preceding chapters, you should have at least general knowledge about similar cases nationwide. All that is left is to ensure that you have baseline knowledge of similar cases that have occurred within your jurisdiction. This is what this chapter is about: how to set up a database application so that you can access and cross-tabulate information from prior cases to help you draw substantive conclusions about open files.

CHOOSING THE SOFTWARE

The first step in setting up any database application is the choice of software. Currently there are many database applications on the market that will suit most needs, ranging in price from $100 to $400. Although any of these software titles should allow you to perform the type of analysis described here, we recommend one of the xbase-brand database systems, because these will allow you to transport your data to any other software application. If you cannot acquire an xbase-brand database package, it is in your best interest to use a package that can translate its native file format to xbase. Some of the more popular xbase software applications are dBASE III+, dBASE IV, and FoxPro version 2 or greater.

In this chapter we will illustrate how to set up a sample database application in FoxPro. We choose this application for two reasons: First, we believe that it is one of the best database managers available at an affordable price; second, its command syntax is highly compatible with that of dBASE III+ and dBASE IV.[1]

THE BASICS

Before we begin, a bit of background information regarding xbase systems may be useful. Xbase systems were first pioneered by C. Wayne Ratliff, a programmer who worked for the Viking Lander Project at NASA in the mid-1970s. Ratliff patented his first database application, called Vulcan, in 1978. Overwhelmed by orders for the product, Ratliff sold the marketing rights to Ashton-Tate in 1980. Ashton-Tate then improved Ratliff's program through the addition of commands and screens and renamed it dBASE II. Because this application was the first of its kind, Ashton-Tate took the lead in the database software industry and set the standard for everyone else to follow.

Xbase systems are generally referred to as *row-format* database managers, whereas spreadsheet applications are generally conceived of as column-based applications. In an xbase system, every new case (every new offender, in this instance) has a new record or row, and within each row is a series of fields or columns known as *database fields*. These database fields may be character, numeric, date, or memo fields.

- *Character fields* may contain a mix of alphanumeric letters or numerals. These fields are generally used for persons' names, addresses, or the names of specific programs. These fields cannot be used to compute sums or averages or for any other numerical computation.
- *Numeric fields* are used to enter and reference numerical integers. Alphanumeric letters cannot be entered into numeric fields. These fields can be used to compute sums, totals, or averages on a set or subset of fields.
- *Date fields* are used to enter specific dates in time. Like numeric fields, date fields will not accept alphanumeric letters. With date fields, one can compute the time between two dates. For example, one can compute the number of days, months, or years an offender was incarcerated before reoffending.
- *Memo fields* are used to store paragraphs of free-form text. These fields may be used, for example, to store comments on a given offender. These fields are not limited to any particular character space.

In addition to the fields described above, the program asks the user to define the amount of space the program should assign to each field. When you define the structure of a database file, the program prompts you to specify the number of spaces or columns it should reserve for each field. For instance, for a field defined as a victim name field, 25 characters is usually sufficient. If you reserve too many character spaces for a field, the file will take up space that could be better used elsewhere. The only two types of fields for which you do not need to specify the number of columns to be reserved are the date and memo fields. Date fields by default are assigned 8 columns; memo fields appear on the surface to take up 10 columns, and their only space limitation is contingent on the availability of space on the storage medium (i.e., hard or floppy disk).

MENU SYSTEMS AND COMMAND STRUCTURE

We now turn to the task of creating a database application. Even though FoxPro and dBASE share similar file formats, there are some subtle differences between them. The most striking for database beginners is their menu systems. Luckily, the end user does not have to use the built-in menu system, but can rely on direct commands entered from the command or dot prompt. Because of the differences in the menu systems of the two software programs, we will perform all our tasks from the dot or command prompt.

If you are using dBASE III+ or dBASE IV, hit <Escape>, and the program should return you to a blank screen with a period in the bottom left corner. If you are using FoxPro, press <Control> and <F2> simultaneously to get the prompt that will allow you to enter commands directly into the system.

The first task is to create a database to hold the information we have; for simplicity's sake, we assume in this chapter that you are interested in entering information on victims only. The first step is to type the command

```
CREATE VICTIM 8
```

followed by <Enter> (all commands typed at the command prompt are followed by <Enter>). This simple command will create a new database called VICTIM.DBF and bring up a data field definition screen in which you are prompted to enter your field names, characteristics of each field, and the number of columns or spaces you wish the program to assign to each field. This screen should appear similar to that shown in Figure 11.1.

For our sample application we have decided that our database should include a collection of demographic information on the victim and the facts of the criminal event. Suppose that a law enforcement agency assigns a 12-character case number to every violent criminal episode, consisting of the year of the crime, the district in which it occurred, and the investigating officer's badge number, with the elements separated by dashes (or hyphens). This

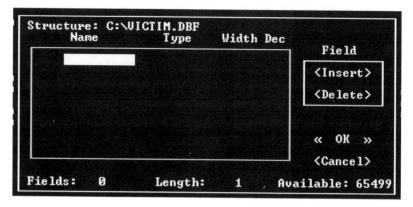

Figure 11.1

field we call <CASEID>. In this example our case ID number is
94-DIST4-311. Because this field consists of a mixture of numerals
and alphanumeric letters, the field type has to be character. So, to
define the first field we enter the name CASEID and press <Enter>.
Under the field type column, we type the first letter of the kind of
field we wish to use, in this case C, for character field, and the cursor
automatically jumps to the field width column. To define the number
of columns we should reserve for this field, we enter 12 and press
<Enter>. The cursor then automatically scrolls to the next definable
field.

The second field in this sample application will be used to record
the date the offense occurred. We name this field DATEOFF. As
before, we type DATEOFF in the name for the second field and use
the tab key to go to the field type column. To define this as a date
field, we type D, and the program automatically assigns it a width
of 8. Again, the cursor jumps to the name column for the next
definable field.

We may also be interested in capturing the age of the victim when
the crime occurred, so we name the next field VICTAGE. We type
in the name and use <Tab> or <Enter> to go to the field type column.
Because this field is composed entirely of whole integers, it should
be designated a numeric field. Therefore, we type N and the cursor

moves to the field width column. Because it is possible for a victim in the sample to be over the age of 99, we define this field with a width of 3 and press <Enter>. The program then prompts us to enter the number of decimal places we wish to carry this field to. Because we will be recording only age by whole years here, we enter 0 or simply hit <Enter> to move onto the next field.

The fourth field we will enter in this application is a written narrative detailing the known facts of the case. This field may be used as a catchall for interesting facts that are not captured in quantifying data. This field we call FACTS. As before, we enter the name of the field in the appropriate space and use <Tab> to go to the field type column. Because we want this field to be in free format without limitation on space, we define it as a memo field by entering M. The program automatically assigns the field a width of 10 and then moves the cursor to the name definition column for user-definable field 5.

At this point we have defined four fields of differing types. These four fields are clearly not enough, however, to contain all the information we will need to be able to draw any substantive conclusions about the characteristics of our victims in a selected number of violent crimes. For the sake of this exercise, we will enter three more fields: race of the victim, gender of the victim, and type of offense either completed or attempted against the victim. The field for the race of the victim, which we name RACE, should have a column width of at least 10 to accommodate all possible racial descriptions. The field named GENDER we assign a width of 6, to allow room to type *male* or *female*. The final field, which we call OFFENSE, we assign a width of 20, to allow for a few descriptive words. At this point our screen looks like the one in Figure 11.2.

We are now finished defining our database structure and wish to exit and save these settings. To do this in FoxPro, hold down <Control> and press <Enter>. If you are using a version of dBASE, hold down <Control> and press <End>. The dBASE program will then ask you if you wish to append new records; for the moment, type N to exit back to the command prompt.

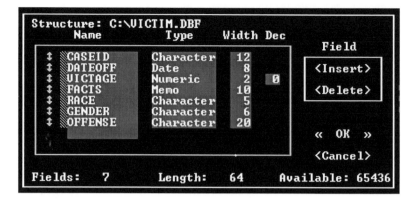

Figure 11.2

We have now successfully created our own sample database application consisting of seven fields of differing types. To make changes in the database structure, you can type MODIFY STRUC-TURE at the dot prompt and make the necessary modifications. This command can also be used to add or delete fields as needed. When you are finished with any structural modification, remember to hit the appropriate exit and save command (FoxPro, <Control> + <Enter>; dBASE, <Control> + <End>).

ADDING NEW RECORDS

Now that we have the database defined to our specifications it is time to enter some cases. However, before we can enter any data we must first access or open the database file we have just created. To open a database from the dot prompt in either FoxPro or dBASE, type

USE VICTIM 8

The database is now open and ready to use. We next add or append a blank record at the bottom of the database and enter our new data into this row. To accomplish this task we issue two commands:

```
Caseid   94-DIST4-311
Dateoff  06/01/94
Victage  47
Facts    Memo
Race     WHITE
Gender   FEMALE
Offense  INDECENT EXPOSURE

              VICTIM.FACTS
 THIS VICTIM WAS ASLEEP IN HER HOME WHEN THE
 ASSAILANT FORCIBLY ENTERED THE HOUSE AND EXPOSED
 HIMSELF TO HER.  WHEN THE VICTIM SCREAMED, THE
 ASSAILANT LEFT IMMEDIATELY, LAUGHING LOUDLY AND
 SCREAMED THAT HE WOULD BE BACK
```

Figure 11.3

```
APPEND BLANK 8
EDIT 8
```

An empty data entry screen should appear in which our field names are listed down the left-hand side. The data on a given victim can now be entered in the appropriate fields. To follow along with this tutorial, begin in the first field and fill in the information provided in the screen shown in Figure 11.3. You will find that accessing the memo field requires some additional steps. In both FoxPro and dBASE, you must press <Control> and <Page Down> simultaneously to bring up a text edit screen in which the free-form text for this field can be entered. <Control> + <W> in FoxPro and <Control> + <Page Up> in dBASE returns you to the previous screen.

When you finish entering the case data, exit the database and save your new revisions by pressing <Control> and <End> simultaneously. Congratulations—you have successfully entered your first case into the database.

For the sake of this exercise, you should enter in several more cases to see how you may use this database application to query for possible offender patterns. Enter the cases shown in the screens in Figures 11.4 and 11.5 in your database. Remember, you must append a blank record and edit that blank record by issuing the following commands:

```
Caseid   94-DIST3-252
Dateoff  04/19/94
Victage  28
Facts    Memo
Race     WHITE
Gender   FEMALE
Offense  INDECENT EXPOSURE

                    VICTIM.FACTS                    ≡
THIS VICTIM WAS ON HER WAY TO WORK WHEN AN
UNKNOWN ASSAILANT OPENED HIS TRENCH COAT AND
EXPOSED HIMSELF TO HER AT 19TH AND BROADWAY AT
4:15 IN THE AFTERNOON.
```

Figure 11.4

```
APPEND BLANK 8
EDIT 8
```

Remember to exit and save by pressing <Control> + <End>.

Congratulations—you have now entered three cases into your database file and are ready to start analyzing the data to look for trends. In the next section we take you on a guided tour of how to structure your database queries to see if there is a pattern for this recent rash of indecent exposures.

QUERYING THE DATABASE FILE

Querying a database is nothing more than asking the program to give you information based on the data stored in the database. The key to making effective use of your database is in knowing how to ask the right questions in the correct format.

Before we begin to show you how to build queries, we want to make a couple of points clear. First, when you ask the program a question about a character field, you must enclose the clause following the field name in quotes. This tells the program that you are searching for a text string. Date fields also must have their own clause delimiters, which appear on the computer keyboard as curly

```
Caseid   94-DIST3-211
Dateoff  04/15/94
Victage  35
Facts    Memo
Race     WHITE
Gender   FEMALE
Offense  INDECENT EXPOSURE
─────────────────── VICTIM.FACTS ───────────────────
THIS VICTIM WAS ON HER WAY TO THE GREENWOOD MALL
SHOPPING WITH HER MOTHER WHEN AN UNKNOWN ASSAILANT
OPENED HIS TRENCH COAT AND EXPOSED HIMSELF TO HER AT THE
BUS STOP AT THE CORNER OF GREENWOOD AND MONTGOMERY ROAD
AT 10:30 AM.
```

Figure 11.5

brackets (e.g., {04/04/94}). Numeric fields do not require any field clause delimiters.

We begin our demonstration of the power of querying your sample database by building a simple query. Suppose you want to ask the program to count, average, or list a specific number of cases or fields that satisfy a particular condition. For example, say you want to know how many indecent exposure cases have been reported. You must pose your query in language that the computer program understands. For xbase applications, this language is the same across different software titles, so instead of having to learn a different language for every program, you have to learn only one—another reason we have chosen to use this type of platform. To ask the program to answer the question just proposed, type the following command:

```
COUNT FOR OFFENSE="INDECENT EXPOSURE"  8
```

This simple query should return a value of 3. You may also want to know how many of the victims have been white. To ask, type:

```
COUNT FOR RACE="WHITE"  8
```

Such simple counts are excellent for tallying raw statistics at the end of a quarter or year, but they really tell us little about the profile of a violent or sex offender. We really need to focus more specifically on a subset of victims. Say, for instance, we want to know how many females have been victims of some type of indecent exposure. The command for such a query would include an "and" clause to include more conditions. This particular command would look like this:

```
COUNT FOR GENDER="FEMALE" AND
OFFENSE="INDECENT EXPOSURE" 8
```

We could also easily include many more conditions in which we may be interested, such as race and time frame. In such a case we may be interested in determining the number of cases of indecent exposure that happened to white females since April 4, 1994. The command for this database query would look like this:

```
COUNT FOR GENDER="FEMALE" AND RACE="WHITE"
AND OFFENSE="INDECENT EXPOSURE" AND
DATEOFF >={04/04/94} 8
```

Once you get the hang of the language structure of your database application, you can ask it to give you facts and figures on anything you want to examine regarding the data stored within it.

THE AVERAGE COMMAND

The average command works much like the count command except that the field you are querying must be in a numeric format (obviously, people's names and offense types cannot be averaged). Say that you are interested in determining the average age of the victims in your database. You would issue the following command:

```
AVERAGE VICTAGE 8
```

If you want to focus on a subset of the sample, the command would be more complex. For example, if you want to know the average age of only the white, female victims, your command would be as follows:

```
AVERAGE VICTAGE FOR RACE="WHITE" AND
GENDER="FEMALE" 8
```

A more complicated query regarding the average age for all the white, female victims of indecent exposure prior to April 6, 1994, would require the following command:

```
AVERAGE VICTAGE FOR RACE="WHITE" AND
GENDER="FEMALE" AND OFFENSE="INDECENT
EXPOSURE" AND DATEOFF < {04/06/94} 8
```

THE LIST COMMAND

In structure, the list command mirrors the two commands described above. However, a list query does not ask the program to compute a new value or answer, but simply to list the variables specified. Say you want to view the facts and dates of offense for every indecent exposure case. The command would appear as follows:

```
LIST DATEOFF, FACTS FOR OFFENSE="INDECENT
EXPOSURE" 8
```

For all of the commands described here, the output is sent to the screen by default. However, the user can also specify that the output to be sent to the printer with the inclusion of a "to printer" clause. For example, if you want the results of the preceding query printed out, the command would appear as follows:

```
LIST DATEOFF, FACTS FOR OFFENSE="INDECENT
EXPOSURE" TO PRINT 8
```

COMPLEX DATA ANALYSIS

As the above discussion shows, querying a database is a straight-forward task. All you have to know is how to ask the program the right questions in the correct syntax. However, there may be times when you want to take a more in-depth look at the data and compute some sample nonparametric statistics. FoxPro has the power to accomplish this type of task, but using it requires relatively exten-sive programming skills. The beauty of FoxPro's xbase format is that almost every new-generation statistical package also includes an xbase translator. This permits the user to read and write xbase files directly to and from that package.

Most novice users do not have the resources to buy such a statistical analysis package, but they usually may acquire what they need in the form of "shareware" that is downloadable from computer bulletin boards across the United States. Several programs are available in this way that will facilitate the computation of such basic statistics as cross-tabulations, chi-squares, correlations, and multiple regression estimates. One of these programs is called XTab, and it is available free of charge on most local computer bulletin boards (the registered version may be ordered from Quality Data Systems for a nominal fee; phone [503] 371-8210).

CONCLUSION

We began this chapter by noting that in order to profile violent criminal offenders successfully, an investigator needs three things: the availability of all the facts of the case, a general knowledge of similar cases nationwide, and a knowledge of similar cases that have occurred within his or her own jurisdiction. In this chapter we have been concerned with helping you to acquire the third of these, by describing how to set up and query a database designed to track crimes of violence committed within your own community. We have demonstrated the techniques and procedures involved in creating a database and the command syntax you need to employ in asking the program questions about the stored data. It is our hope that we have saved you the many valuable hours you may have spent with a complicated user's manual in getting started with the creation of your own database.

Our sample application has been very limited in scope, but we hope that your personal applications will be more detailed, including all of the relevant fields you may require to make in-depth analyses of the crimes you want to study. Any computer-aided analysis will be only as good as the data entered into the system. A good rule of thumb in creating a database is that if you think you will ever need a database field, include it. This may at some point save you hours, if not days, if you need later to locate and input fields that you once thought unimportant.

NOTE

1. Differences between the command structure of FoxPro and dBASE within this sample application come into play only in the case of the menu system and field delimiting clauses. dBASE requires a period before and after an "and" clause; it also requires you to change the format of date fields for use in queries. If you use or plan to use dBASE, consult your user's guide.

12. The Victim in Psychological Profiling

Perhaps no single element in the profiling process has been neglected more than the victim. However, the Behavioral Science Unit of the FBI has been active in securing data regarding the social and behavioral characteristics, as well as the reputations, of victims. These are crucial to the profiling enterprise.

The victim is the last person to witness the crime. If alive, the victim can tell a great deal about the crime. If the victim is deceased, however, the crime scene must tell the story. In either instance, the profiler should be as interested in the activities of the victim as in any element of the submitted packet of information accompanying the request for a profile. It has been noted that victim profiles and information on victims' activities are often neglected in police reports.

ELEMENTS IN THE VICTIM PROFILING PROCESS

It would be remiss to attempt to appraise a crime without some knowledge of the victim, but, unfortunately, the available victim information is frequently lacking in substance. The usual report a profiler receives from a law enforcement agency contains varying degrees of information about the type of weapon used, the position of the victim's body, the amount and type of physical evidence, the autopsy, and other important elements. It is equally important for the profiler to have information concerning the victim's lifestyle, habits, oddities, friends, and so on. Ideally, the profiler should have the following specific information about each victim:

- Physical traits
- Marital status
- Personal lifestyle
- Occupation
- Education
- Personal demographics
- Medical history
- Psychosexual history
- Criminal justice system history
- Last activities

PHYSICAL TRAITS

Perhaps the most important victim element, from a profiling standpoint, is the victim's physical description. Much care must be taken in gathering an accurate description of the victim's basic physical characteristics. Age, for example, can be a critical victim selection factor. For example, Jerry Brudos, a serial killer and serial rapist from Oregon, consistently selected young women, ages 19 to 23, as his victims.

Whether a victim is male or female is often the overarching element in the selection process. Because the young and women are typically among the most vulnerable possible victims, they are often victimized. In our own contacts with serial rapists and murderers, many have related their conscious efforts to select victims based on those individuals' perceived vulnerability.

The way a person dresses may be included in the category of physical appearance. For some offenders, the victim's way of dressing has some significance. For example, one serial murderer chose his particular victims because he said that "they looked like hookers." None of the four young women he abducted and killed were prostitutes, but in the killer's mind they *appeared* to be prostitutes. Their style of dress signaled to him their "vocation" and, in effect, resulted in their deaths.

Hairstyle and hair color may also play roles in victim selection for the violent personal offender. For example, Ted Bundy was reportedly fond of college-aged women with long, dark hair parted in the middle (lighter-haired victims Laura Aime and Susan Rancourt were exceptions).

MARITAL STATUS

As much information as possible should be collected about the victim's marital status. Too often, investigators will note on a report simply "married"; this fact alone does not provide much information. One case of which we are aware serves as an illustration of the importance of understanding the state of a victim's marriage. The nude body of a woman was found along a rural road. She had been shot five times, and had not been raped. Police were told that she had been happily married for 15 years. She and her husband were reportedly regarded as pillars of their community and very community-minded. They had no children. The woman had been employed, and she was known to be athletic; she went to an exercise center two evenings a week. By all outward appearances, her marriage was committed and happy.

During the investigation, the homicide detectives were told that the woman was an introvert and had no close friends and no enemies. The profiler who consulted on the case pointed out the inconsistent nature of this information. It seemed odd that an attractive, athletic young woman would have no known close friends. The detectives eventually discovered several leads as a result of the suspicion that, regardless of how it appeared, all was not well within the victim's marriage. Closer investigation revealed a husband with a very jealous disposition and a wife with an outside love interest. One small, seemingly insignificant statement signaled an inconsistency that led to the successful resolution of the case.

PERSONAL LIFESTYLE

A victim's daily activities can yield vital information concerning his or her character that may serve as an index not only of the type of people who compose the victim's circle of friends, but the many others with whom he or she may have come into contact. The victim's hobbies, sports interests, drug use, tendency to frequent bars or other types of gathering spots, drinking habits, and so on, as well as any recent changes in his or her behavior or personality, may also be significant.

Many victims have significant others who can serve as sources of such information. These contacts should be queried regarding any sudden or recent changes in the social life or personality of the victim. Such information may be useful in establishing not only the victim's availability, but his or her susceptibility.

OCCUPATION

A victim who has been employed has an expanded network of relationships, both professional and personal. These relationships should be examined, even though the number of people involved may be quite large. A careful examination of all persons who had frequent contact with the victim through the workplace may lead to a better understanding of the victim's personality as well as to information about any organizations to which the victim belonged.

Any special training or education demanded by the victim's occupation may provide clues to any organizations, associations, conferences, or meetings in which the victim may have been active. The people who join or attend such groups usually have common interests, and these interests can provide further insight into the victim's personality and vulnerability.

Investigators should also be careful to research a victim's past jobs, in case he or she had a network of friends, enemies, or acquaintances there who might provide more information.

One case with which we are familiar provides an example of the importance of gathering information on a victim's employment history. A young woman was killed by repeated stabs to the neck. In the setting where she had worked for the past 7 years, one of her fellow workers remarked to investigators that a male coworker of the victim's had tried unsuccessfully to date the woman. Also, the victim had once stated to another person that if anything ever happened to her, "John would probably be the one to kill me." By interviewing the victim's fellow workers, investigators developed two viable leads.

EDUCATION

It is important to take into account not only the extent of the victim's education, but also the various schools and programs he or she attended. As with occupation, education widens the network of acquaintances. For example, it has been reported that Ted Bundy was in the same psychology class at the University of Washington as Lynda Ann Healy, one of his victims (this has not been verified by university officials, but has been reported in several different sources). In a 1987 interview with the first author, Ann Rule, author of a book about Bundy (see Rule, 1980), again noted this, and also related that Lynda had shopped at the same grocery where Bundy had worked as a stock boy, two blocks from where she lived and was killed. As a law student living on a college campus, Bundy was able to associate with young women who would be vulnerable and easy to kill.

The intelligence of the victim may also serve as an indicator of the type of people with whom he or she associated. The assumption may be that a relatively intelligent victim may be likely to associate with others of like intelligence. This may be especially important when an attack that appears to have been process focused has taken place away from the victim's home.

Of course, many victims are victims of opportunity, taken by offenders after only minimal stalking. Such a victim's level of education would not necessarily have much significance for the investigation. The more stalking of the victim is evident, the more helpful are certain kinds of information about him or her.

PERSONAL DEMOGRAPHICS

The location of the victim's home may play an important role in the manner in which he or she became a victim. Crime rates in general tend to be higher in particular neighborhoods, and if a victim resides in such a neighborhood, this can be valuable information.

The locations of a victim's past residences may indicate whether he or she tends to live in certain areas out of preference or necessity. Also, useful information may be obtained from a thorough canvassing of the neighborhoods in which a victim has previously lived. Past neighbors and friends can lend an appraisal of the victim's lifestyle and circle of friends. Particular names coming up repeatedly in the investigation may indicate continuing relationships.

The investigator should be aware of the complexity of the victim's neighborhood, including its racial composition. Most rapists and murderers tend to choose victims of their own races, so if the racial composition of the victim's neighborhood is radically different from the victim's race, several possibilities arise that may account for the victim's living in a particular area.

MEDICAL HISTORY

One obvious benefit of looking into a victim's medical history is that it may reveal information that could connect the victim to the perpetrator, such as evidence of a communicable disease. For instance, it was stated in one interview that one of Ted Bundy's early victims had gonorrhea; however, he did not test positive for this disease.

The dental records of an unidentified deceased victim can lead to identification; sometimes this is the only reliable means of doing so, especially if the body is in an advanced state of decomposition. For example, dental records proved invaluable in the identification of Susan Rancourt, an alleged Bundy victim, when her body was found a year after she had been reported missing.

The mental health history of a victim may also supply valuable information, both about the victim's possible psychological state and about other persons with whom the victim could have come into contact. It may also serve as an indicator of whether the behavior exhibited by the victim was consistent with his or her daily life and activities. Some behavior may be commonplace for some people but quite inappropriate in others.

PSYCHOSEXUAL HISTORY

All people have some unrealistic fears, although some have more than others. Some people are afraid of high places, some are afraid to ride in elevators, and so on. Investigators should attempt to find out about any such fears on the part of the victim from his or her friends, relatives, and acquaintances. Such information may aid in the creation of a more complete personality profile of the victim.

The victim's sexual history might also provide a clue to the present crime. For example, the victim in one case was known to have dated several men, to have taken showers with them, and to have been involved in mutual oral sex and masturbation with them, but would not have coitus because she wanted to "save herself" for her future husband. This was important information that opened up an additional avenue for investigation in the case.

It is also important for the profiler to assess the victim's personality. As we have noted, the personality is the sum total of what a person is. It is not static; although it does not usually change in its essential nature, the personality undergoes some changes over time. A personality profile of the victim should be developed from current sources and compared with one developed from sources outside the present time frame. An examination of the victim's personality will help the profiler to draw a picture of the types of associates with whom he or she may have been involved or to whom he or she may have been exposed. The importance of a full understanding of the victim's personality cannot be stressed too strongly.

CRIMINAL JUSTICE SYSTEM HISTORY

The victim's history with the criminal justice system, if any, is just as important an element as an understanding of the type of person the victim was. Indeed, the criminal justice history of the victim may be an important indicator of his or her personality. The investigator should find out about any arrest records, court appearances (as defendant, victim, or witness), and pending cases in which the victim has been involved.

LAST ACTIVITIES

In the development of any psychological profile, special attention should be directed to the victim's activities prior to the crime itself. Routes of travel, social activities, phone calls, meetings attended or missed, and anything that appears to be outside the victim's usual pattern of daily living should be noted (Holmes & De Burger, 1988, p. 90). In other words, the investigator should ask, Did the victim do something unique before the crime that alerted someone to his or her vulnerability and availability?

CONCLUSION

In this chapter we have attempted to offer some insight into the role of the victim as it relates to the crime itself. Whatever daily activities, lifestyle, interaction with the criminal justice system, and other social and psychological elements are associated with the victim, even if these are offensive to the profiler or in conflict with his or her personal values, the profiler must view the victim as an integral component in the profiling process. The victim is part of the crime that has been committed, and just as the crime scene, the body disposal site (in a murder case), particular words used by the perpetrator during the crime, and other factors all have import for the profiling process, an understanding of the victim must be added to the total picture.

13. Profiling and the Future

The future of psychological profiling appears promising. The number of cases profiled over the past decade has risen dramatically, and, once viewed with great suspicion, profiling is now being judged increasingly by police professionals as a useful addition to the tools available in the battle against crime.

Of course, there are many who are still reluctant to accept profiling as a reliable and useful tool. Godwin (1978), for example, asserts that profiling has served little purpose in solving crimes: "Nine out of ten of the profiles are . . . vapid. They play at blindman's bluff, groping in all directions in the hope of touching a sleeve. . . . They [the police] require hard data: names, faces, fingerprints, locations, times, dates. None of which the psychiatrists [profilers] can offer" (p. 276). He goes on to describe profiles themselves as dull and more than a little tedious, a position shared by Campbell (1976). Levin and Fox (1985) have asserted that psychological profiles are of little use in the identification of murderers: "Unfortunately, this tool, no matter how expertly implemented, is inherently limited in its ability to help solve crimes" (p. 175).

As we have noted, profiling is best considered a starting point for the investigation of particular crimes; we make no claim that it should stand on its own as the sole forensic tool used in criminal cases.

ADDITIONAL USES FOR PROFILING

Historically, the preponderance of requests submitted to the FBI's Criminal Personality Profiling Program have sought aid in murder cases (65%) and rape cases (25%) (Howlett, Hanfland, & Ressler, 1986). Other kinds of crimes account for the remaining requests: cases involving child molestation, kidnapping, extortion, obscene telephone calls, suicide, and other criminal activity.

Profiles have been developed for many different kinds of offenders, as well as for other categories of actors. Haran and Martin (1984), for example, have developed an interesting profile of armed bank robbers in which they list the following social core variables for these offenders: young (age 26-30), white (61%), unemployed (56%), and high school dropouts (49%); only 15% have no criminal record, and fewer than one in four acts alone. Rider (1980a, 1980b) has developed a typology of arsonists based on psychological profiling. Casey-Owens (1984) argues that the letters of anonymous letter writers should be examined utilizing a psycholinguistic approach; this researcher distinguishes among the types of such letter writers using the following categories: threatening, obscene, racial, extortion, nuisance, stool pigeon, and guilty conscience.

Such novel uses of profiling apart from the 90% that is concerned with murder and rape cases, as mentioned above, may indicate that the practice has gained some recognition and appreciation for its usefulness in the resolution of certain crimes and in the investigation of other phenomena. As it gains acceptance, the use of profiling will undoubtedly become more widespread, and in addition to its application to murder and rape cases it will be used routinely to help investigators deal with such offenders as obscene letter writers and phone callers, arsonists, and even bank robbers.

EDUCATION AND TRAINING FOR PROFILING

There is nothing magical or mysterious about the art of psycho-logical profiling. As academicians, we are always amazed when we hear a student say, "The professor really knows his stuff. He must be really smart—I can't understand what he is saying." On the contrary, we believe that a truly intelligent professor is careful to teach in a manner that is intelligible to students. Academicians and other professionals are infamous for creating jargon that protects their knowledge—as well as their status—from close examination. This is true of many fields and disciplines, including medicine, psychiatry, psychology, and law enforcement, and it has recently emerged in profiling. There are some who would like others to believe that profiling can be done only by a select few who have special and unique education and training somehow gained through osmosis as a result of close association with the "masters."

Our message here is that profiling can be done by many different people. Touted "authorities," many of whom sit behind desks hun-dreds of miles away from the crime investigations on which they consult, may lend insight into certain crimes, but there is no prepon-derance of empirical evidence to support the position that police investigators with some knowledge of the social and behavioral sciences cannot just as reliably profile their own cases. Many have done so on a small scale for years. In seminars held across the nation, the first author always stresses that profiling can and should be done by those who are closest to the crimes: the police. Again, we emphasize: There is nothing mysterious about the profiling process.

To develop a profile of the perpetrator of a serious, violent crime, one needs to have knowledge of sociology, psychology, psychiatry, and criminology, and the ability to blend the theories of these disciplines. No one has a monopoly on such knowledge. Common sense combined with sound social and behavioral concepts can yield valuable and reliable results. Unfortunately, sometimes law enforce-ment turf issues hinder the profiling process, and sometimes the successful resolution of a case is impeded by the disease referred to as NIH—"not invented here."

COMPUTERIZED MONITORING

The computer revolution has arrived in law enforcement, as it has in almost every other facet of our lives. The Drug Enforcement Administration, for example, now uses a computerized tracking system called the Drug Abuse Warning Network (DAWN). This program monitors drug mentions in police records in 26 standard metropolitan statistical areas across the nation. The Automated Reports and Consummated Orders System (ARCOS) yields the data necessary for estimating drug-related law enforcement requirements and alerts investigators to sources of diversion in the illicit drug distribution chain. By combining DAWN and ARCOS, the DEA is able to disseminate information on drug abuse and trafficking trends to law enforcement agencies across the United States.

In New York, the Homicide Assessment and Lead Tracking System (HALT) has been established by the Division of Criminal Justice Services and the Division of State Police. HALT's mission is to collect case data on nondomestic homicides in the state of New York and then disseminate the information within the state. In 1983, Michigan implemented the Homicide Investigative Tracking System (HITS), a statewide computerized system to collect data on homicides that is analogous to the HALT system in New York. When similar crimes are matched up by the system, related police agencies are notified.

The Violent Criminal Apprehension Program (VICAP) of the National Center for the Analysis of Violent Crime has been in operation since the late 1980s. This ambitious program has the goal of collecting nationwide data and analyzing specific violent crimes (Howlett et al., 1986). As Pierce Brooks (1981), a former homicide detective and currently a consultant to the FBI, has noted:

The lack of a centralized automated computer information center and crime analysis system to collect, collate, analyze and disseminate information from and to all police agencies involved in the investigation of similar pattern multiple murders, regardless of the date and location of occurrence, is the crux of the problem. (p. 201)

VICAP deems appropriate those cases involving (a) solved or unsolved homicides or attempts, especially those that involve an abduction, are apparently random, motiveless, or sexually oriented, or are known or suspected to be part of a series; (b) missing persons, where the circumstances indicate a strong possibility of foul play and the victim is still missing; and (c) unidentified bodies when the manner of death is known or suspected to be homicide (Howlett et al., 1986, pp. 15-16).

The officials involved in VICAP are hopeful that the program will be expanded to include rape, child sexual abuse, and arson cases. Part of this hope may lie in the fact that the program has not attracted the volume of cases that the FBI had anticipated (Howlett et al., 1986, p. 17). To help combat this shortfall, VICAP's administrators shortened and revised the questionnaire that agencies must fill out for cases to be analyzed.

There are few empirical data yet available to support the validity of the results yielded by VICAP; nevertheless, the program could be a valuable starting point for the accumulation of information regarding certain kinds of crime. As noted above, however, turf issues can sometimes interfere with the success of such efforts; these must be resolved before VICAP and other similar programs can be truly successful.

The computer should be viewed as a powerful technological tool that can aid in crime investigation; it is not a substitute for human intelligence or for a solid investigation of crimes by competent law enforcement personnel. What a computer issues after a run of data depends on the design of the program used and the data input; thus, great care should be taken in the handling of data. Further, the key to the efficacy of the computer is the validity of the data input.

COMPUTERIZED PROFILING

Although the profiling process is in part an art that can be practiced only by humans, in the near future a computerized profiling program might help law enforcement personnel to define quickly and efficiently the types of personalities associated with such violent crimes as lust murder, rape, and serial murder. Certainly, the examination of a crime scene requires a human element, but computers can be used to analyze the data accumulated by humans and to summarize the analysis in a series of statements that can provide some basic information about an unknown suspect. A profiler makes calculated, educated guesses—these are more than wild guesses, but they are guesses nonetheless. A computer program can be used to collate information and even to notify other police agencies participating in similar cases and offer them the same personality profiles.

The design of any computer program developed to create offender profiles must take into account all of the information outlined in this volume—that is, all the same information that is important in "traditional" profiling. The crime scene elements, personality characteristics, deviant behaviors, everyday activities, and other factors associated with violent criminals will be vital components of any such program. The authors of such a program must be aware of and theoretically fluent in the concepts of profiling, as well as the disciplines of psychology, sociology, psychiatry, and criminology. Indeed, the authorship of such a program would be best achieved through the joint endeavor of investigators, theoreticians, and computer-literate professionals.

CONCLUSION

The computer revolution is having a dramatic influence on the criminal justice system. Computers have been used for some time now by law enforcement for storage of records, personnel files, and criminal files; for case management; and for management of fiscal matters. Computers are also now being used to track crimes and criminals. Psychological profiling would seem to be the next logical task for the computer. The human art of profiling can benefit from the speed and accuracy of analysis that computer technology represents.

Profiling is finally coming of age in the battle against violent crime. We have stressed in this volume not only the components of profiling, but the need for profiling itself. As we noted in Chapter 1, a profile can narrow the range of effort, identify suitable interrogation techniques, and help with the evaluation of the unknown suspect's personal belongings. Profilers should make use of all available, legitimate resources, including sociological, psychiatric, psychological, and criminological theory; the experiences and expertise of law enforcement officials; and computer technology. The computer may be the next major advance in our arsenal of weapons against crime.

Suggested Further Reading

Apsche, J. (1993). *Probing the mind of a serial killer.* Morrisville, PA: International Information Associates.

Balken, S., Berger, R., & Schmidt, J. (1983). *Crime and delinquency in America.* Belmont, CA: Wadsworth.

Barlow, H. D. (1981). *Introduction to criminology.* Boston: Little, Brown.

Bartol, C. R. (1985). *Criminal behavior: A psychological approach.* Englewood Cliffs, NJ: Prentice Hall.

Baumann, E., & O'Brien, J. (1993). *Murder next door.* New York: Diamond.

Biondi, R., & Hecox, W. (1992). *The Dracula Killer.* New York: Pocket Books.

Brussels, J. A. (1968). *Casebook of a criminal psychiatrist.* New York: Bernard Geis.

Conradi, P. (1992). *The Red Ripper.* New York: Dell.

Danto, B. L., Bruhns, J., & Kutcher, A. (Eds.). (1982). *The human side of homicide.* New York: Columbia University Press.

Eckert, A. (1985). *The scarlet mansion.* Boston: Little, Brown.

Eitzen, D., & Timmer, D. (1985). *Criminology: Crime and criminal justice.* New York: John Wiley.

Gaynor, J., & Hatcher, C. (1987). *The psychology of child firesetting.* New York: Brunner/Mazel.

Graysmith, R. (1976). *Zodiac.* New York: Berkeley.

Groth, N., & Birnbaum, H. (1979). *Men who rape: The psychology of the offender.* New York: Plenum.

Healy, W., & Bronner, A. (1985). *New light on delinquency and its treatment.* New Haven, CT: Yale University Press.

Hunt, D. (1993). *Practical criminal investigation.* Placerville, CA: Copperhouse.

James, E. (1991). *Catching serial killers.* Lansing, MI: International Forensic Services.

Jones, V., & Collier, P. (1993). *True crime: Serial killers and mass murderers.* Forestville, CA: Eclipse.

Julian, J., & Kornblum, W. (1986). *Social problems.* Englewood Cliffs, NJ: Prentice Hall.

Kinder, G. (1982). *Victim.* New York: Dell.

Knox, D. (1984). *Human sexuality.* St. Paul, MN: West.

Larsen, R. (1980). *Bundy: The deliberate stranger.* New York: Pocket Books.

Lillyquist, M. (1980). *Understanding and changing criminal behavior.* Englewood Cliffs, NJ: Prentice Hall.

Nettler, G. (1982). *Explaining criminals.* Cincinnati, OH: Anderson.

Olsen, J. (1993). *The misbegotten son: A serial killer and his victims.* New York: Delacorte.

Sanders, W. W. (1980). *Rape and women's identity.* Beverly Hills, CA: Sage.

Schwartz, A. (1992). *The man who could not kill enough.* Secaucus, NJ: Carol.

Siegel, L. (1986). *Criminology.* St. Paul, MN: West.

Stack, A. (1983). *The Want-Ad Killer.* New York: Signet.

Stack, A. (1984). *The I-5 Killer.* New York: Signet.

Swanson, C., Chamelin, N., & Territo, L. (1977). *Criminal investigation.* Santa Monica, CA: Goodyear.

Terry, M. (1987). *The ultimate terror.* Garden City NY: Doubleday.

Weston, P., & Wells, K. (1990). *Criminal investigation: Basic perspectives.* Englewood Cliffs, NJ: Prentice Hall.

Wolfgang, M., Figlio, R., & Sellin, T. (1972). *Delinquency in a birth cohort.* Chicago: University of Chicago Press.

References

Abel, G., Lawry, S., Karstrom, E., Osborn, C., & Gillespie, C. (1994). Screen tests for pedophilia. *Criminal Justice and Behavior, 21,* 115-131.

Abrahamsen, D. (1944). *Crime and the human mind.* New York: Columbia University Press.

Aichorn, A. (1935). *Wayward youth.* New York: Viking.

American Psychiatric Association. (1994). *Diagnostic and statistical manual of mental disorders* (4th ed.). Washington, DC: Author.

Amir, M. (1971). *Patterns in forcible rape.* Chicago: University of Chicago Press.

Barret, G. (1990). *Serial murder: A study in psychological analysis, prediction, and profiling.* Unpublished master's thesis, University of Louisville, KY.

Baumann, E. (1991). *Step into my parlor.* New York: Bonus.

Becker, J., & Abel, G. (1978). Men and victimization of women. In J. Chapman & M. Gates (Eds.), *Victimization of women.* Beverly Hills, CA: Sage.

Bennett, W., & Hess, K. (1994). *Criminal investigation* (4th ed.). Minneapolis: West.

Blackburn, D. (1990). *Human harvest: The Sacramento murder story.* New York: Knightsbridge.

Blair, D. (1993). The science of serial murder. *American Journal of Criminal Law, 20*(2), 1-12.

Bradway, W. (1990, September). Stages of sexual assault. *Law and Order,* pp. 119-124.

Brantingham, P., & Brantingham, P. (Eds.). (1981). *Environmental criminology.* Beverly Hills, CA: Sage.

Briere, J., & Runtz, M. (1989). University males' sexual interest in children: Predicting potential indices of "pedophilia" in a nonforensic sample. *Child Abuse & Neglect, 13,* 65-75.

Brooks, P. R. (1981). *Vi-CAP.* Unpublished manuscript.

Brownmiller, S. (1975). *Against our will: Men, women and rape.* New York: Simon & Schuster.

Burg, B. (1983). *Sodomy and the perception of evil.* New York: New York University Press.

Burgess, A. W., Groth, A., & Holmstrom, L. L. (1978). *Sexual assault of children and adolescents.* Lexington, MA: Lexington.

Cahill, T. (1986). *Buried dreams: Inside the mind of a serial killer.* New York: Bantam.

Campbell, C. (1976, February). Portrait of a mass killer. *Psychology Today, 9,* 110-119.

Carr, C. (1994). *The alienist.* New York: Random House.

Casey-Owens, M. (1984). The anonymous letter writer: A psychological profile? *Journal of Forensic Sciences, 29,* 816-819.

Cason, H. (1943). The psychopath and the psychopathic. *Journal of Criminal Psychopathology, 4,* 522-527.

Classifying sexual homicide crime scenes. (1985). *FBI Law Enforcement Bulletin, 54,* 12-17.

Cleckley, H. (1982). *The mask of sanity.* New York: Plume.

Cohen, M., Garofalo, M., Boucher, B., & Seghorn, T. (1971). The psychology of rapists. *Seminars in Psychiatry, 3,* 307-327.

Connors, C. (1992, May 9). Priests and pedophilia: A silence that needs breaking? *America,* pp. 400-401.

Cox, M. (1991). *The confessions of Henry Lee Lucas.* New York: Pocket Star.

Craig, D. P. (1980). *Hip pocket guide to planning and evaluation.* Austin, TX: Learning Concepts.

Crime scene and profile characteristics of organized and disorganized murderers. (1985). *FBI Law Enforcement Bulletin, 54,* 18-25.

DeHaan, D. (1991). *Kirk's fire investigation* (3rd ed.). Englewood Cliffs, NJ: Prentice Hall.

Dettlinger, C., & Prugh, J. (1984). *The list.* Atlanta, GA: Philmay.

Dollard, J., et al. (1939). *Frustration and aggression.* New Haven, CT: Yale University Press.

Douglas, J., & Burgess, A. (1986). Criminal profiling: A viable investigative tool against violent crime. *FBI Law Enforcement Bulletin, 55,* 9-13.

Douglas, J., Burgess, A. W., Burgess, A. G., & Ressler, R. (1992). *Crime classification manual.* Lexington, MA: Lexington.

Doyle, A. C. (1891a). The Bascombe Valley mystery. In *The original illustrated Sherlock Holmes.* Secaucus, NJ: Castle.

Doyle, A. C. (1891b). A case of identity. In *The original illustrated Sherlock Holmes.* Secaucus, NJ: Castle.

Doyle, A. C. (1891c). The five orange pips. In *The original illustrated Sherlock Holmes.* Secaucus, NJ: Castle.

Doyle, A. C. (1891d). The red headed league. In *The original illustrated Sherlock Holmes.* Secaucus, NJ: Castle.

Doyle, A. C. (1892). The man with the twisted lips. In *The original illustrated Sherlock Holmes.* Secaucus, NJ: Castle.

Drukteinis, A. (1992). Serial murder: The heart of darkness. *Psychiatric Annals, 22,* 532.

Dunham, R., & Alpert, G. (1993). *Critical issues in policing: Contemporary readings.* Prospect Hills, IL: Waveland.

Durkheim, E. (1965). *The division of labor in society* (G. Simpson, Trans.). New York: Free Press.

Egger, S. (1990). *Serial murder: An elusive phenomenon.* New York: Praeger.

Ferrero-Lombroso, G. (1911). *Criminal man, according to the classification of Cesare Lombroso.* New York: Putnam.

Fisher, S. (1962). The MMPI: Assessing a famous personality test. *American Behavioral Scientist, 6,* 20-21.

Forehand, R., Wierson, M., Frame, C., Kempton, T., & Armistead, L. (1991). Juvenile firesetting: A unique syndrome of an advanced study of antisocial behavior? *Behavioral Research Therapy, 29,* 125-128.

Frank, G. (1966). *The Boston strangler.* New York: Signet.

Freeman-Longo, R., & Wall, R. (1986, March). Changing a lifetime of sexual crime. *Psychology Today,* pp. 58-64.

Freud, S. (1948). Criminals from a sense of guilt. In *The standard edition of the complete psychological works of Sigmund Freud* (J. Strachey, Ed., Trans.). London: Hogarth.

Freund, K., & Watson, R. (1992). The proportions of heterosexual and homosexual pedophiles among sex offenders against children: An exploratory study. *Journal of Sex and Marital Therapy, 18,* 34-38.

Gammage, J. (1991, September 8). Serial murders are on the rise, say experts. *Philadelphia Inquirer,* p. A1.

Ganey, T. (1989). *St. Joseph's children: A true story of terror and justice.* New York: Lyle Stuart/Carol.

Geberth, V. (1981). Psychological profiling. *Law and Order, 29,* 46-49.

Geberth, V. (1993). *Practical homicide investigation: Tactics, procedures, and forensic techniques* (2nd ed.). Boca Raton, FL: CRC.

Gibbs, N. (1991, June 3). When is it rape? *Time,* pp. 48-54.

Gibney, B. (1990). *The beauty queen killer.* New York: Pinnacle.

Gilbert, J. (1986). *Criminal investigation.* Columbus, OH: Charles E. Merrill.

Glick, L. (1995). *Criminology.* Boston: Allyn & Bacon.

Glueck, S., & Glueck, E. (1950). *Unraveling juvenile delinquency.* Cambridge, MA: Harvard University Press.

Godwin, J. (1978). *Murder USA: The ways we kill each other.* New York: Ballantine.

Gold, L. (1962). Psychological profile of the firesetter. *Journal of Forensic Sciences, 7*(4), 406.

Groth, A., & Burgess, A. W. (1980). Male rape: Offenders and victims. *American Journal of Psychiatry, 137,* 806-810.

Groth, A., Burgess, A. W., & Holmstrom, L. L. (1977). Rape, power, anger and sexuality. *American Journal of Psychiatry, 134,* 1239-1243.

Haas, L., & Haas, J. (1990). *Understanding sexuality.* St. Louis, MO: C. V. Mosby.

Hagan, F. (1986). *Criminology.* Chicago: Nelson-Hall.

Haran, J., & Martin, J. (1984). The armed bank robber: A profile. *Federal Probation, 53,* 47-53.

Harris, G. (1994, March 10). Children still fascinate molester, 82. *Courier Journal,* pp. A1-A5.

Harris, T. (1981). *The red dragon.* New York: Putnam.

Hazelwood, R. (1994, March). [Lecture delivered at the Southern Police Institute]. Ft. Lauderdale, FL.

Hazelwood, R., & Warren, J. (1989, January). Serial rapists. *FBI Law Enforcement Bulletin.*

Hertica, M. (1991, February). Interviewing sex offenders. *Police Chief,* pp. 39-43.

Hickey, E. (1991). *Serial murderers and their victims.* Pacific Grove, CA: Brooks/Cole.

Hirschi, T. (1969). *The causes of delinquency.* Berkeley: University of California Press.

Holmes, R. M. (1973). *Sexual behavior: Homosexuality, prostitution and swinging.* Berkeley, CA: McCutcheon.

Holmes, R. M. (1983). *The sex offender and the criminal justice system.* Springfield, IL: Charles C Thomas.

Holmes, R. M. (1988). A model of personal violence. *Kentucky Research Bulletin, 2,* 1-5.

Holmes, R. M. (1991). *Sex crimes.* Newbury Park, CA: Sage.

Holmes, R. M., & De Burger, J. (1985). Profiles in terror: The serial murderer. *Federal Probation, 39,* 29-34.

Holmes, R. M., & De Burger, J. (1988). *Serial murder.* Newbury Park, CA: Sage.

Holmes, R. M., & Holmes, S. T. (1992). Understanding mass murder: A starting point. *Federal Probation, 56,* 53-61.

Holmes, R. M., & Holmes, S. T. (1994). *Murder in America.* Thousand Oaks, CA: Sage.

Holt, F. (1994, March). The arsonist's profile. *Fire Engineering,* pp. 127-128.

Home Box Office. (1984). *Murder: No apparent motive* [film]. Stamford, CT: Vestron Video.

Howlett, J., Hanfland, K., & Ressler, R. (1986). The violent criminal apprehension program. *FBI Law Enforcement Bulletin, 55,* 14-18.

Icove, D. (1990, December). Serial arsonists: An introduction. *Police Chief,* pp. 46-48.

Jackman, T., & Cole, T. (1992). *Rites of burial.* New York: Pinnacle.

Jeffers, H. (1992). *Who killed Precious?* New York: St. Martin's.

Jenkins, P. (1994). *Using murder: The social construction of serial homicide.* New York: Aldine de Gruyter.

Jenkins, P. (1995). A historical perspective on serial murder: England, Germany and the USA 1900-1940. In T. O'Reilly-Fleming & S. Egger (Eds.), *Serial and mass murder: Theory, research, policy.* Toronto: University of Toronto Press.

Johnston, S., French, A., Schouweiler, W., & Johnston, F. (1992). Naivete and need for affection among pedophiles. *Journal of Clinical Psychology, 48,* 620-627.

Kelley, C. (1976). *Uniform crime reports: Crime in the United States.* Washington, DC: Government Printing Office.

Kennedy, D., & Nolin, R. (1992). *On a killing day.* New York: Bonus.

Kenney, J., & More, H. (1994). *Principles of investigation.* Minneapolis: West.

Knight, R., Carter, D., & Prentky, R. (1989). A system for the classification of child molesters. *Journal of Interpersonal Violence, 4,* 3-23.

Knight, R., & Prentky, R. (1987). The developmental antecedents and adult adaptations of rapist subtypes. *Criminal Justice and Behavior, 14,* 403-426.

Kolarik, G. (1992). *Freed to kill: The true story of serial murderer Larry Eyler.* New York: Avon.

Kolko, D., & Kazdin, A. (1992). The emergence and recurrence of child firesetting: A one-year perspective study. *Journal of Abnormal Child Psychology, 20,* 17-36.

Langer, W. (1972). *The mind of Adolph Hitler.* New York: New American Library.

Law, D. (1991, January). The pyromaniac vs. the professional hired torch. *Fire Engineering,* pp. 50-53.

Leo, J. (1993, October 11). Pedophiles in the schools. *U.S. News & World Report,* p. 37.

Levin, J., & Fox, J. (1985). *Mass murder: America's growing menace.* New York: Plenum.

Lewis, N., & Yarnell, H. (1951). Pathological firesetting (pyromaniac). *Nervous and Mental Disease Monographs, 2.*

Linedecker, C., & Burt, W. (1990). *Nurses who kill.* New York: Windsor.

Linz, D. (1989). Exposure to sexually explicit materials and attitudes toward rape: A comparison of study results. *Journal of Sex Research, 26,* 50-84.

Lunde, D. (1976). *Murder and madness.* New York: W. W. Norton.

Lynch, K. (1960). *The image of the city.* Cambridge: MIT Press.

Margolin, L. (1994). Child sexual abuse by uncles: A risk assessment. *Child Abuse & Neglect, 18,* 215-224.

Macy, J. (1979). To the reader. In *Arson: The federal role in arson prevention and control* [report to the Congress]. Washington, DC: Federal Emergency Management Agency U.S. Fire Administration, Office of Planning and Evaluation.

Merton, R. (1968). *Social theory and social structure.* New York: Macmillan.

Michaud, S. (1986, October 26). The FBI's new psyche squad. *New York Times Magazine.*

Michaud, S., & Aynesworth, H. (1983). *The only living witness.* New York: Signet.

National Center for Missing and Exploited Children. (1985). *Child molesters: A behavioral analysis.* Washington, DC: Author.

Neitzel, M. (1979). *Crime and its modification: A social learning perspective.* Elmsford, NY: Pergamon.

Norris, J., & Birnes, W. (1988). *Serial killers: The growing menace.* New York: Dolphin.

O'Brien, D. (1985). *Two of a kind: The hillside stranglers.* New York: Signet.

Okami, P., & Goldberg, A. (1992). Personality correlates of pedophilia: Are they reliable indicators? *Journal of Sex Research, 29,* 297-328.

Orr, J. (1989, July). Profiles in arson: The vanity firesetter. *American Fire Journal,* pp. 24-47.

Pallone, N., & Hennessy, J. (1992). *Criminal behavior: A process psychological analysis.* New Brunswick, NJ: Transaction.

Palmiotto, M. (1994). *Criminal investigation.* Chicago: Nelson-Hall.

Patchen, D., & Bodiford, S. (1978, February). [Interview with Ted Bundy, audiotape]. Pensacola, FL.

Porter, B. (1983, April). Mind hunters. *Psychology Today,* pp. 1-8.

Proulx, J., Cote, H., & Achille, P. (1993). Prevention of voluntary control of penile response in homosexual pedophiles during phallometric testing. *Journal of Sex Research, 30,* 140-147.

Queen's Bench Foundation. (1976). *The rapist and his crime.* New York: John Wiley.

Quinsey, V., Chaplin, T., & Upfold, D. (1990). Arsonists and sexual arousal to firesetting: Correlation unsupported. *Journal of Behavioral Therapy and Experimental Psychiatry, 20,* 203-209.

Rada, T. (1978). Alcoholism and forcible rape. *American Journal of Psychiatry, 32,* 444-446.

Ressler, R., Burgess, A., & Douglas, J. (1988). *Sexual homicide.* Lexington, MA: Lexington.

Ressler, R., & Shachtman, T. (1992). *Whoever fights monsters.* Lexington, MA: Lexington.

Rice, M., & Harris, G. (1991). Firesetters admitted to a maximum security psychiatric institution. *Journal of Interpersonal Violence, 6,* 461-475.

Rider, A. (1980a). The firesetter: A psychological profile [Part 1]. *FBI Law Enforcement Bulletin, 49,* 7-17.

Rider, A. (1980b). The firesetter: A psychological profile [Conclusion]. *FBI Law Enforcement Bulletin, 49,* 5-11.

Rossmo, D. (1994). Place, space, and police investigations: Hunting serial violent criminals. In J. E. Eck & D. A. Weisburd (Eds.), *Crime prevention studies* (Vol. 4). Monsey, NY: Criminal Justice Press.

Rossmo, D. (1995). Targeting victims: Serial killers and the urban environment. In T. O'Reilly-Fleming & S. Egger (Eds.), *Serial and mass murder: Theory, research, policy.* Toronto: University of Toronto Press.

Rossmo, D. (in press). Target patterns of serial murderers: A methodological model. *American Journal of Criminal Justice.*

Rule, A. (1980). *The stranger beside me.* New York: Signet.

Russell, D. E. H. (1982). *Rape in marriage.* New York: Macmillan.

Sakeheim, G., & Osborn, E. (1986). A psychological profile of juvenile firesetters in residential treatment: A replication study. *Child Welfare, 65,* 495-503.

Sakeheim, G., Vigdor, M., Gordon, M., & Helprin, L. A. (1985). Psychological profile of juvenile firesetters in residential treatment. *Child Welfare, 64,* 453-476.

Samenow, S. (1984). *Inside the criminal mind.* New York: Time Books.

Sanders, L. (1981). *The third deadly sin.* New York: Berkeley.

Sanders, W. (1983). *Criminology.* Reading, MA: Addison-Wesley.

Sapp, A., Huff, T., Gary, G., Icove, D., & Horbert, P. (n.d.). *A report of essential findings from a study of serial arsonists.* Unpublished manuscript.

Schechter, H. (1990). *Deranged.* New York: Pocket Books.

Schwendinger, J., & Schwendinger, H. (1983). *Rape and inequality.* Beverly Hills, CA: Sage.

Sears, D. (1991). *To kill again.* Wilmington, DE: Scholarly Resources.

Sharn, L., & Glamser, D. (1994, March 24). One man, more than 100 fires: Seattle area's wave of terror. *USA Today,* p. 9A.

Shook, L. (1990). Sexual glossary. In L. Shook, *Investigation of variant sex styles.* Montgomery, AL: Auburn University Press.

Smith, C., & Guillen, T. (1990). *The search for the Green River Killer.* New York: Onyx.

Stack, A. (1983). *The lust killer.* New York: Signet.

Stea, D. (1969). The measurement of mental maps: An experimental model for studying conceptual spaces. In K. R. Cox & R. G. Golledge (Eds.), *Behavioral problems in geography* (pp. 228-253). Evanston, IL: Northwestern University Press.

Sullivan, T., & Maiken, P. (1983). *Killer clown.* New York: Pinnacle.

Sutherland, E. (1937). *The professional thief.* Chicago: University of Chicago Press.

U.S. Department of Justice, Bureau of Justice Statistics. (1988). *Report to the nation on crime and justice* (2nd ed.). Washington, DC: Government Printing Office.

U.S. Department of Justice, Bureau of Justice Statistics. (1991). *Criminal victimization in the United States.* Washington, DC: Government Printing Office.

U.S. Department of Justice, Bureau of Justice Statistics. (1992). *Criminal victimization in the United States.* Washington, DC: Government Printing Office.

U.S. Department of Justice, Bureau of Justice Statistics. (1993). *Sourcebook of criminal justice statistics, 1993.* Washington, DC: Government Printing Office.

U.S. Department of Justice, Federal Bureau of Investigation. (1993). *Uniform crime reports for the United States: Crime in the United States, 1992.* Washington, DC: Government Printing Office.

U.S. Department of the Treasury, Bureau of Alcohol, Tobacco and Firearms. (1992). *1992 explosive incidents report.* Washington, DC: Government Printing Office.

Webb, N., Sakeheim, G., Towns-Miranda, L., & Wagner, C. (1990). Collaborative treatment of juvenile firesetters: Assessment and outreach. *American Journal of Orthopsychiatry, 60,* 305-309.

Yochelson, S., & Samenow, S. (1976). *The criminal personality.* New York: J. Aronson.

Index

About the Authors

Ronald M. Holmes is Professor of Justice Administration at the University of Louisville. He is the author or coauthor of several books, including *Serial Murder*; *Sex Crimes*; *Murder in America*; *Criminology: Policies, Issues, and Research*; *Sexual Behavior*; and *The Sex Offender and the Criminal Justice System.* He has also published extensively in scholarly and law enforcement journals, including *Police Chief, New England Journal of Criminal Justice, Contemporary Journal of Criminal Justice, American Journal of Criminal Justice,* and *Law and Order.* He is the past editor of the *American Journal of Criminal Justice.* He has assisted police departments across the United States with more than 425 homicide and rape investigations. He has also consulted with many U.S. police departments and police in several other countries and has appeared on national and international television shows to speak about sex crimes and serial and mass homicide. A deputy coroner in Kentucky, he is also vice president of the National Center for the Study of Unresolved Homicides, Inc. Many of the cases the center has worked on have benefited from the profiling concepts outlined in this book.

Stephen T. Holmes is a doctoral student at the University of Cincinnati. He has published in several scholarly journals, including the *American Journal of Criminal Justice* and the *Contemporary Journal of Criminal Justice,* as well as in such periodicals as *Federal Probation* and *Law and Order.* He is coauthor, with Ronald M. Holmes, of *Murder in America.* He has conducted research in the areas of female homicide, drug use and crime, murder rates, and parole and probation issues. He is scheduled to receive his doctoral degree in criminal justice in 1995.

D. Kim Rossmo is the Detective Inspector in charge of the Vancouver Police Department's Geographic Profiling Unit. A 16-year veteran, he has worked various assignments including patrol, emergency response, crime prevention, organized crime intelligence, and offender profiling. He holds a Ph.D. in criminology from Simon Fraser University where he teaches courses on policing and serial murder. He has researched, lectured, and published in the areas of geographic profiling, serial murder, environmental criminology, and problem-oriented policing. He is currently Executive Vice-President of the Canadian Police Association.